What's in a Scottish Placename?

Compiled by Peter Terrell

Illustrated by Elfreda Crehan

Published 2016 by Lexus Ltd
60 Brook Street, Glasgow G40 2AB

Compiled by Peter Terrell
Cover design, page design, maps and illustrations by Elfreda Crehan

Thanks are due to Steven Ritchie for his work on the Gaelic
pronunciation in this compilation and for his invaluable comments on
the improbability of certain mooted derivations.

www.lexusforlanguages.co.uk

British Library Cataloguing in Publication Data
A catalogue record for this book is available from the British Library.
ISBN: 978-1-904737-391
Printed and bound in Latvia by Dardedze hologrāfija

Contents

Introduction

J ust down the road from here is a row of new houses called *Willow View Court*. When the houses were first built a couple of years ago there was not a willow in sight. And neither had there been, in living memory. A few willow trees have since been planted to justify the name. The Scottish town of *Glenrothes* was built in the mid 20th century. It is not in a glen. There is no glen in it. There is no glen near it. Nor is there any known relationship with a glen. Unlike the development of Willow View Court there is little here that can be done to justify the name. *Braehead Shopping Mall* is not on or near the head of a brae. The list goes on.

These three names were chosen for their appeal and are, in respect of their origin, more akin to personal names or product names. Emotive and evocative appeal is something which a very great many Scottish placenames undeniably have. There are exceptions, of course: *Campbeltown, Sandhole*. But then we have the odd, the amusing and the romantic.

If you stop to think about them, some placenames, mostly taken for granted, are odd, extremely odd: *Bathgate, Carstairs, Boysack, Stove*.

Other placenames cause amusement. Who can travel around Scotland and not be amused when passing a sign for *Bonkle, Stuck, Minnigaff, Twatt, Glenbucket, Dull, Brawl*?

Yet other names have a ring of romance and adventure: *Lochinvar, Ardnamurchan, Achnamara, Lairig Ghru*.

It is not the case that the ancestors of modern Scots were imbued with a love of romantic names or of names with comic overtones. In a great number of cases the romantic name hides a mundane meaning, the comic ring distorts a blunt naming reality. Modern names (*Willow View Court, Glenrothes, Braehead*) take over the emotive aspect of a name without regard to reality. Many ancient names, if translated *back* into their original sense, would be totally unsuitable for the modern world. Not many new estates, new villages or townships would fall back on any of the following typical meaning elements that lie disguised in Scottish placenames: field, bend, ditch, bog.

What led to the creation of old names? Some of the main causes for the name of a place coming into being can be identified as

natural geographical feature (rock, bay, height, hollow, bog, hazel tree patch)

ownership (Björn's island, Geirhildr's place)

dedication (Helensburgh, Kilmartin)

human purpose (enclosed bit of land, crossing place, pig field, sheep island)

and far less frequently *aesthetic aspect or allusion* (breast, beautiful).

Rivers have the oldest names. Rivers were boundaries, offered protection, were means of transport, supplied plentiful fish, and, since they flowed endlessly, were sometimes seen as being inhabited by divine spirits. The meanings of river names are hard to determine. It seems that their names point to an older vocabulary that spread across Europe (Scottish Earn and Deveron being possibly related to Rhine and Rhône). Where two or more rivers came together settlements developed and the inhabitants named them by simple description. *Aber* is a fairly commonly found Celtic placename element for the place where two watercourses meet, though it is commoner in Wales than in Scotland. The Scottish equivalent is *inver*, from Gaelic *inbhir* (pronounced in-yuhr in modern Gaelic, the older Gaelic pronunciation of inver having faded). Inver means confluence, a meeting of rivers or streams or a place where a watercourse meets the sea and it is an element that has generated many Scottish placenames. The word 'confluence' itself did not make it as a placename element in Britain, where pre-established Gaelic and Brittonic took precedence over Latin imports. (The Latin *confluentes* did, however, enter into placenaming in other parts of Europe with, for example, *Koblenz* in Germany and the French town of *Confolens*). In all these there is a common feature: initial reference to a significant geographical situation and then adaptation of the underlying naming element to fit the local speech patterns and accents. The tradition has continued with the not particularly evocative placename of *Watermeetings* in South Lanarkshire.

This book takes a look at some 1200 Scottish placenames, a tiny proportion of the national total. To start with, placenames were chosen for inclusion on the basis of their appeal (as words) and of their interest. The size of the named place was not a consideration in the selection. The roadless maps in this book do not distinguish larger towns or cities from small hamlets. Some erstwhile would-be larger human settlements did not manage to progress beyond the stage of tiny hamlet or smallholding and are nowadays perhaps no more than a disused cowshed or a roundabout or a bit of ground with an odd pile of stones. But the name may be of interest.

What exactly is it that makes so many Scottish placenames so distinct, what accounts for the appeal they have, especially to an English-speaker coming from outside Scotland? What is it that has made many Scottish placenames seem like precious antiques, almost like familiar, solid, owned parts of the physical landscape, so much so that you can often hear the natives take a quiet delight in the simple act of uttering a placename? There are four big linguistic influences that have created Scottish placenames. These are Brittonic-Pictish/Cumbric, Old English, Old Norse and Gaelic.

Brittonic-Pictish and Cumbric

Brittonic (also formerly spelled as Brythonic) is a name given by scholars to the Celtic language that was thought to have been the main language spoken in Scotland (and Britain) around 2000 years ago and that stayed in use for some 800 years. There is very little evidence for this language, other than in the names of places. If only the ancient Britons up on and around Dumbarton Rock on the Clyde had recorded their daily experiences. If only the Picts in eastern Scotland had written something down on parchment they could have stolen from the Romans, as well as leaving their beautiful but mysterious inscriptions in stone. The language called Cumbric is thought to be a later development of Brittonic and is a likely forerunner of modern Welsh. However, it is not the object of this book to investigate the original languages spoken in Scotland or to attempt an analysis of the difference between Brittonic-Pictish and Cumbric. In this book the name Cumbric is used to describe the origins of placenames in the southern regions of Scotland, from west to east, and up to the Forth-Clyde line. Brittonic and Brittonic-Pictish are used as more general terms and are used to describe the origins of placenames north of this Forth-Clyde line. As a consequence some name elements will be variously accounted for as either Brittonic-Pictish or as Cumbric, which is not contradictory, but a recognition of the fact that the difference between the two is very probably more geographical than linguistic and that languages do not have precise boundaries on the ground. Examples of name elements that are described as either Brittonic or Cumbric, depending on their location are: *coed* meaning wood, *tref* meaning settlement, *mig* meaning bog, *caer* meaning fort, *cardden* meaning thicket.

Old English

Anyone travelling east from Edinburgh, and looking at the placenames on roadsigns, will soon have the strange impression of having left Scotland and of having landed suddenly in the Weald of Kent or some other part of England. *West Linton, East Linton, Haddington, Whitburn* are all names also found in England and clear evidence of the presence of the old Angles pushing northwards from the Kingdom of Northumbria, often only to be pushed back again by their northern neighbours. With such constant ebb and flow over hundreds of years it was quite natural that the words used by the people of the day would mix, as did their speakers. Many Anglo-Saxon or Old English words became assimilated into what is now known as Scots. Old English *stan* is Scots *stane*, Old English *burna* is Scots *burn*. And the overlaps go further: Old English *lin* is clearly cognate with Gaelic *lion*.

Old Norse

From some time in the 9th century Norsemen began sailing across to Shetland and Orkney, along the north coast of Scotland to Cape Wrath and then down the west coast, setting up home in the Western Isles, on the west coast and continuing on down to Dumfries and Galloway (and beyond to the Isle of Man). Danes were more active on the east coast, and the term Old Norse is used to include names of probable Danish origin. Norsemen have a reputation as raiders and pillagers and the Vikings certainly were. But they were also settlers and made a big impact on Scottish placenames. Typical Old Norse naming elements include *bólstaðr* (farm or homestead), *ey* (island) and *vík* (bay). But often these naming elements mutated when confronted with the languages of contemporary or subsequent natives who spoke another tongue. *Vík* would become Wick or, on the west coast, –uig. *Bólstaðr* would mutate into –bister, –bost, –busta, –ster.

Gaelic

It is said by some that the Gaelic language was introduced to the west of Scotland from Ireland. Against this is the theory that Ireland, its northeast corner in particular, taken together with the southwest of Scotland form a much more natural community than do the west and the east of Scotland, in particular the eastern parts of Scotland that lie above the Forth-Clyde line. The water that separates southwest Scotland from northeast Ireland would have served as a means of maritime communication and ship-borne commerce and interaction, thus not so much separating as joining the two regions. The mountains that divide the west of Scotland from the east of Scotland would have acted as a barrier and severe disincentive to communication and commercial interaction on any significant scale. So it is possible to conjecture that the Gaelic language developed in tandem in Ireland and in Scotland, but as with so many other related languages (Swedish/Norwegian/Danish for example) grew apart to some extent, developed their own structures, vocabulary items and accents, while remaining to a high degree mutually intelligible.

In the descriptions of placenames in this book the term 'old Gaelic' is also used. The lower-case o is deliberate. There is no recorded old Gaelic as there is Old English or Old Norse (apart from some 12th century monks' marginal notes in the 10th century *Book of Deer*). But there are words that have gone out of use in modern Gaelic whose existence is traceable in placenames. An example is the word *lann* (an enclosure, often the land around a church). And interestingly this word, and others, also appear in the vocabularies of other ancient languages, *lann* being Cumbric too, with the same meaning.

But in this mix of language influences is there not one missing? What of Latin? The Romans came to Scotland, built a wall across it, established camps. And just a few of these camps have left their mark in the form of a name with *chester*, an element so frequently found in England but much less so in Scotland. Some references to Latin influence in placenames are made in the descriptions in this book, but they are not extensive enough to constitute a main linguistic naming source. The Romans left linguistically little.

These four main language groups can be unearthed in Scottish placenames like linguistic strata. Down the centuries a good deal of mixing and modification of these strata has taken place. Speakers of one language would, over the years, modify a name to suit their own language, their own way of pronouncing things. Some modifications were slight: Norse *vík* (bay) turning into Gaelic –*uig*. Sometimes, however, the modification was blatant: *King Edward* was superimposed on Gaelic *Cinn Eadaradh* with sovereign disregard for the original simple meaning. It was doubtless here just a question of what the recording scribe could cope with. Other modifications let names slip unnoticed and without demur into the realm of the meaningless and rather ridiculous: Cumbric *Baedd Coed* (boar wood) turning into *Bathgate*. Other modifications stack synonymous linguistic strata one on top of the other. *Quinish Point* was Norse *Kví Nes* (cattle pen point). The Gaels modified the *–nes* to their own way of pronouncing it, which, when written in English, is *–nish*. But *nes* (pronounced nish), which means point, being meaningless to incoming monolingual English-speakers was expanded with the naming word 'point' so as to give it its meaning back.

Placenames which have no obvious meaning are often the ones that have greatest appeal. The names themselves are important. Name a hill, a river, and it ceases to be mere rock or water; it stands now in relation to people. Name a place and that place becomes a reference; it enters into our known and denoted world.

Pronunciation
Gaelic

This book gives a pronunciation guide for names that derive from Gaelic. In some instances this shows a straightforward enough pronunciation path: baile beag (little town) [baluh bek] gives Balbeg. In other cases an English pronunciation has come to be superimposed on the Gaelic: port leathan (broad port) [porsht leh-huhn] gives Portlethen (but there is no th sound in Gaelic). In a very few instances the actual Gaelic pronunciation has held firm in spite of, and to the confusion of, English-speakers: srath abhainn (river valley) [stra avin] gives Strathaven pronounced [stray-ven].

Special Gaelic sounds are: G from the back of the throat, K like the Scottish ch in loch, uh like the e sound in butter.

Old Norse

Old Norse special characters (in this book) are ð a th sound as in the or those, þ a th sound as in thing or thesis, æ as the a in cat, í as the ee in sheet, ǫ as the o in hot or lot. An accent over a vowel lengthens it.

Map Symbols

Picts   *pre-history*   *Romans*   *distillery*   *castle*   *battle*   *abbey*

Shetland

Muckle Flugga

MUCKLE FLUGGA

UNST

FETLAR

● Isbister   YELL

Toft ●
● Sullom Voe   OUT SKERRIES

MAINLAND   ● Skaw Taing

● Voe   Sodom ●   WHALSAY

PAPA STOUR

● Aith
Twatt ●
Walls ●   ● Girlsta

Tingwall ●
● Lerwick
Scalloway ●   BRESSAY

FOULA   Hamnavoe ●   ● Quarff

Stove ●   MOUSA

Fitful Head ●
● Sumburgh

FAIR ISLE

Aith

From Old Norse *eið* which means isthmus or a tongue of land.

Bressay

From Old Norse *brjóst* (breast) and *ey* (island). That's what the Norsemen saw when they looked at it.

Fair Isle

Beautiful no doubt but not by name. A possible origin is a little more down-to-earth: Old Norse *fær* means sheep.

Fetlar

Fetlar is known as the Garden of Shetland. One theory for the origin of the name links its fertile soil to the Norse *fet* (rich, fertile). Another links it to a Norse word *fetlar* meaning straps and suggests that the prehistoric Funzie Girt, a wall which divides the island north to south, was such a marked feature that the incoming Norsemen saw this island as made up of two islands held together by the straps of the Funzie Girt.

Fitful Head

There are two possibilities here, both Old Norse. The Old Norse word *fit* names the webbing on a bird's foot; and *fugl* means bird. Alternatively there is *hvítr* (white) and *fjall* (hill). So this could be either Seabird Head or Whitehill Head.

Foula

From Old Norse *fugl* (bird) and *ey* (island).

Girlsta

The –sta ending goes back to Old Norse *staðr* meaning dwelling or homestead. The Girl– is from Geirhildr, a Viking explorer's daughter.

Hamnavoe

From Old Norse *hǫfn* (harbour) and *vágr* (bay, inlet).

Isbister

From Old Norse *Ine* (a personal name) and *bólstaðr* (homestead or farm).

Lerwick

The main town of Shetland takes its name from Old Norse *leir* (mud) and *vík* (bay). The muddy bay wasn't the main place in Old Norse days though.

> *The Iron-Age Clickhimin Broch is just south of Lerwick.*

> *The old Norse festival, Up-Helly-Aa, takes place here in Lerwick in January every year. Men dressed as Vikings parade through the town with burning torches and set fire to a replica of a Viking longboat.*

Mainland

Old Norsemen called this *megin land*, the main or biggest piece of land.

Mousa

The name is thought to come from a form of Old Norse *mosi* (moss).

> *This little island of Mousa boasts what is most probably the best, most intact surviving Iron-Age broch, built, it is thought, around 100 BC.*

Muckle Flugga

From Old Norse *mikill* (big) plus *flug* (steep rockface) plus *ey* (island), the big referring to the rockfaces rather than the island.

Out Skerries

A *skerry* is a mainly Scottish name for a rocky island or reef.

Papa Stour

Probably from Old Norse *papa* (priest) and *stórr* (great).

Quarff

This is likely to be from Old Norse *hvarf* (shelter, refuge).

Scalloway

Quite likely from Old Norse *skáli* (big cottage or hall) and *vágr* (bay). Scalloway, not muddy Lerwick, was the main place here in Norse days.

Shetland Islands

The traditional view, not shared by all, is that the name comes down from Old Norse *hjalt* (dagger) and *land*, a picture which has some plausibility if the outline of the main island (Mainland) is seen from above. It is also thought that the name might be a Norse adaptation of a name (unknown) that already existed when the colonizers arrived.

Skaw Taing

Taing is from Old Norse *tangi* which is a spit or tongue of land sticking out into the sea. This is a commonly found element in placenames in the Northern Isles. Skaw might be from Old Norse *sker*, a prominent rock, sticking up in the landscape.

Sodom

The name is a (bizarrely) anglicized variant of *sudheim*, an Old Norse word, or rather a word from the Shetland descendant language of Old Norse, Norn. It means southern home. The older version of the name is still in use, presumably because less embarrassing.

The poet Hugh MacDiarmid lived and wrote in Sodom for several years.

Stove

The name is likely to be from Old Norse *stofa* meaning a room (or a cottage) (maybe they were the same thing). The word is cognate with German *Stube* parlour. Possible connotations of comfort and warmth.

Sullom Voe

Old Norse *sulan* means gannets and *vágr* means bay. But another theory is that this comes from a combination of Old Norse *sól* and *heimr* meaning sunny home.

Sumburgh

The burgh is Old Norse *borg* meaning fort. And the Sum– is most probably the time-worn remnant of the personal name of an old Norseman called Sweyn.

Jarlshof, at Sumburgh, has seen some 4000 years of human settlement, from the Bronze Age, Iron Age, through to Norse and medieval times.

Southwest of Sumburgh and on the western prong of this southern tip of Shetland is the Ness of Burgi, an Iron-Age blockhouse built into the headland.

15

Tingwall

This has nothing to do with walls. The –wall is from Old Norse *vǫllr* (field) and the Ting– from Old Norse *þing* (parliament, assembly). This is a field in which people would come together to discuss and decide local issues and administer justice.

Toft

Old Norse *toft* (or *topt*) is a homestead. It can also mean a building site, a place where a settlement had started to grow up.

Twatt

Not a postal address for the status-conscious, perhaps. This is from Old Norse *þveit* meaning clearing or settlement and is related to the English ending *thwaite*. There's another Twatt in Orkney.

Unst

The name may well pre-date the Vikings. But there is a theory that it may go back to Old Norse *ǫrn* (eagle). And the –st could

> *Muness Castle on Unst is the most northerly castle in the British Isles.*

be a trimmed-down form of the common ending –sta, which is itself a trimmed-down form of *bólstaðr* (homestead), though this usually refers to humans. Or again the ending may be from *vist* (dwelling).

Voe

From Old Norse *vágr* (bay).

Walls

No, not walls. It's from Old Norse *vágar* (bays).

> *About a mile east of Walls is Stanydale Temple, the remains of a Neolithic hall.*

Whalsay

From Old Norse *hvals* (of the whale) and *ey* (island).

Yell

Old Norse *geldr* means barren, and is a term used especially of cows that do not yield milk or of female animals that won't have young. Was this a summer grazing place for these?

Orkney

The Old Man of Hoy

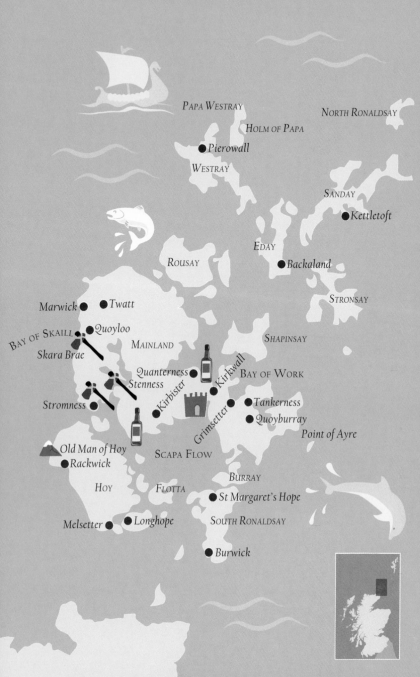

PAPA WESTRAY

NORTH RONALDSAY

HOLM OF PAPA

● Pierowall

WESTRAY

SANDAY

● Kettletoft

EDAY

ROUSAY

● Backaland

STRONSAY

Marwick ●   ● Twatt

SHAPINSAY

BAY OF SKAILL

● Quoyloo

MAINLAND

Skara Brae

Quanterness ●   Kirkwall   BAY OF WORK

Stenness

Kirbister

Stromness ●

Grimsetter   ● Tankerness

● Quoyburray

Point of Ayre

SCAPA FLOW

Old Man of Hoy

● Rackwick

BURRAY

HOY

FLOTTA

● St Margaret's Hope

Melsetter ●   ● Longhope

SOUTH RONALDSAY

● Burwick

Backaland

Old Norse *bakki* is a bank, as in the bank of a stream.

Burray

This means fortified island, or island with a fort on it, and comes from Old Norse *borg* (fort) and *ey* (island).

Burwick

From Old Norse *vík* (bay) and possibly *borg* (fort).

Eday

From Old Norse *eið* (isthmus) and *ey* (island).

Flotta

Possibly from Old Norse *floti* (fleet) and *ey* (island). Although some say it may be from an Old Norse word for flat.

Grimsetter

Kirkwall airport was previously known as Grimsetter, having once been the *sætr* or homestead of a man called Grim, a Norseman.

Holm of Papa

From Old Norse *holmr* (small island) and *papa* (priest). It is thought that the priest would have been a missionary monk.

> *The little island of Holm of Papa has a Neolithic chambered cairn some 3000 years old. The cairn is thought to be a communal burial place.*

Hoy

From Old Norse *hár* (high) and *ey* (island). Say it often enough with an Old Norse sort of accent and you'll get to Hoy.

Kettletoft

An Old Norse *toft* or *topt* is a homestead or a site where building work is going on or has been going on. The man Kettle was presumably the owner of this Orcadian site. A Pictish name *Catel* is known.

Kirbister

The name is thought to come from Old Norse *kirkja* (church) and a contraction of *bólstaðr* (homestead, farm).

Kirkwall

Church wall? No. Old scribes and mapmakers would, not unnaturally, write down a name in a form most familiar to them and in a form most likely to be accessible to others. The wall comes from Old Norse *vágr*, which means bay. And the kirk is from Old Norse *kirkja*. So this is: Church on the bay.

> *The distillery by Kirkwall is Highland Park.*

Longhope

Seize the day? Et spem longam recense? No, this is from Old Norse *hóp*, which is a sheltered bay, and a long one at that.

Mainland

Who would call an island mainland? (Well the mainland is an island too). And seafaring old Norsemen called this *megin land* (the main or biggest piece of land).

Marwick

This could be from Old Norse *már* (seagull) and *vík* (bay).

Melsetter

From Old Norse *melr* (grassy dune) and *setr* (homestead).

North Ronaldsay

The two Ronaldsays don't share a common name origin. This one comes from Old Norse *Ringan* and *ey* (island). Ringan is the Old Norse variant of St Ninian, whose missionary work reached this island.

Old Man of Hoy

The Hoy is Old Norse *hár ey* (high island). But the Old Man is Pictish, from *alt* (high) and *maen* (rock), with the sound of the words – not their meaning – turned into English to give a name rather less pedestrian than High Rock of High Island.

Orkney

Orc is an old Celtic word meaning pig. *Ey* is Old Norse for island. In Old Norse the islands are known as *Orkaneyjar* (seal islands).

Papa Westray

From Old Norse, the western *ey* or island of the *papa* or priest.

Pierowall

The wall is from an Old Norse element *vágr* (bay). And the first part? There is an Orkney and Shetland word peerie (or peedie) which means 'little'. And it is thought that this might be at work in the Piero–. But where it comes from nobody knows. That it could have an Old Norse history too is not a wild assumption.

Point of Ayre

An Old Norse *eyrr* was a spit of land or a beach, the sort of geographical feature that is also called, in English, a point.

Quanterness

The –ness is from Old Norse *nes* (headland). The Quanter– must remain mysterious. It may be quite coincidental that the Old Norse *kvantr* means suffering or loss.

> *Quanterness is the site of a Neolithic chambered cairn, a tomb where evidence of prehistoric mass burials has been unearthed.*

Quoyburray

Quoy– is from Old Norse *kví* (enclosure, cattle pen) and –burray is from Old Norse *borg* (fort) and *ey* (island), whether the reference was to this island or borrowed from the name of the little island of Burray just to the south is not clear.

Quoyloo

The quoy element is from Old Norse *kví* which is an enclosure or a cattle pen. But what of the loo element? This ending in placenames can signify a clearing in woodland. And there was woodland here, it is believed, up till around 1500 BC, a long time before the Norsemen arrived.

Rackwick

This is thought to come from Old Norse *reka* (seaweed) and *vík* (bay).

Rousay

From Old Norse *Hrolfr* (a person's name) and *ey* (island). Old Hrolfr's name being a bit of a mouthful for the later locals, it has been simplified over the centuries.

Sanday

From Old Norse *sandr* (sand) and *ey* (island).

Scapa Flow

This name is more than slightly mysterious. The Flow is fairly straightforward, being from Old Norse *flói* which means a large bay or an open stretch of water. But Scapa? An Old Norse word *skalpr* means sheath or, in related Danish use, a shell. And an old Scots word, *skalp*, recorded in 1536, which has a variant form *scaup*, is a shellfish bed. This place still is a stretch of water good for shellfish.

> *Scapa Flow is where the German fleet was scuttled in 1919. It's the place that launched the slang word 'scarper' – from rhyming slang scapa flow = go = rush off in a hurry.*

Shapinsay

From Old Norse *Hjalpand* (a person's name) and *ey* (island).

Skaill, Bay of

The name is probably from Old Norse *skáli* which can mean either a large cottage or a hall.

Skara Brae

The Skara could be either from a Norse word meaning edge or possibly from a personal name. The only certainty in this name is with the vastly less ancient Scots *brae* (bank, hillside).

> *Skara Brae is the site of the remains of prehistoric dwellings, dating from around 2500-3000 BC at a time when the water here was an inland freshwater loch.*

South Ronaldsay

The two Ronaldsays don't share a common name origin. This one comes from an Old Norse name *Rognvaldr* and *ey* (island). Rognvaldr is equivalent to Scots Ronald.

St Margaret's Hope

Poetic as it sounds, the Hope is not Margaret's hope but comes from Old Norse *hóp* which means (shallow) bay or inlet.

Stenness

From Old Norse *steinn* (stone) and *nes* (headland).

> *The standing stones of Stenness were put in place some 5000 years ago.*

Stromness

From Old Norse *straumr* (current) and *nes* (headland).

> *And about 5 miles northeast of Stromness is the Ring of Brodgar, a Neolithic stone circle.*

> *About 8 miles east of Stromness is the ancient chambered cairn of Maes Howe (a howe being a mound). More than 5000 years old, it bears witness to the building skills of prehistoric man.*

Maes Howe

23

Stronsay

From Old Norse *stjarna* (star) and *ey* (island).

Tankerness

From the old name *Tancred* with Old Norse *nes* (cape, headland).

Twatt

This is from Old Norse *þveit* meaning clearing or settlement and is related to the English ending *thwaite*, which is fairly commonly found in the north of England. There's a Twatt in Shetland too.

Westray

From Old Norse *vestr* (west) and *ey* (island).

Work, Bay of

Could Work be a remnant from the Old Norse personal name, *Wroc*?

Outer Hebrides
~ North

Callanish

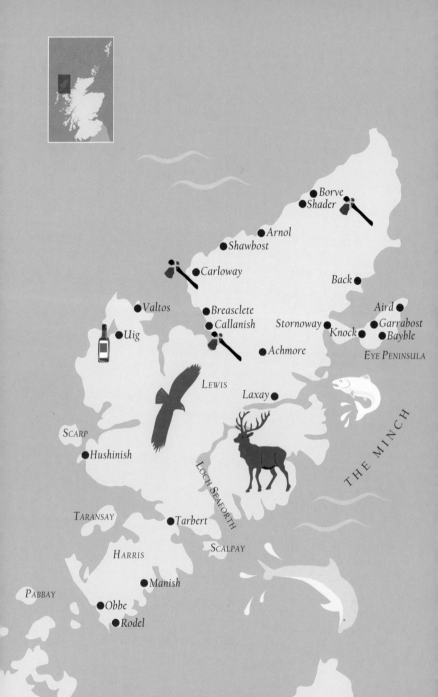

Achmore

From the Gaelic *achadh* [ahK-uhG] (field) and *mòr* (big).

Aird

This is straight Gaelic *àird* [arsht] (headland, height).

An t-Ob

see Obbe

Arnol

This name is said by some to come from Old Norse with the meaning of eagle hill. Old Norse *ǫrn* (eagle) or *ari* (eagle) together with *hallr* (hillside) are the likely naming candidates.

Here at Arnol there is a traditional crofter's blackhouse, restored to show what would have been the typical living quarters for Gaelic-speaking families for many generations back into the past.

Back

Old Norse *bakki* is a bank. Gaelic *bac* means hollow or dip (in the ground). But then you can't have the one without the other. Gaelic *bac* also means peat-bank. The k in the modern name is quite unnecessary, just an oddity of anglicization.

Bayble

Lewis has its own Bayble, the name thought to stem from Old Norse *papa* (priest, monk) and *ból* (farm, homestead).

Borve

From Old Norse *borg* (fort).

Breasclete

From the Old Norse *breiðr áss klettr* (broad-ridge cliff or rocky outcrop).

Callanish

From Old Norse *nes* (headland) preceded by the personal name *Kali*. The final s of *nes* in the mouth of a Gaelic speaker would become sh. The Gaelic name is Calanais.

The spectacular Bronze-Age standing stones of Callanish are some 3000 years old (though some date them much earlier).

Carloway

The name comes down from the Norse *vágr* (bay) and a personal name before that.

There is a well-preserved broch here at Carloway.

Eye Peninsula

From Old Norse *eið*. This is normally translated as isthmus; but here the name refers to the whole peninsula.

Garrabost

From Old Norse *bólstaðr* (homestead, farm) preceded by what could be either Gaelic *gàrradh* [gah-ruhG] (enclosure) or Old Norse *garðr* which also means enclosure.

Harris

From Old Norse *hærri* (higher). The final –s started appearing in records in the late 16th century.

Harris is famous for the tweed (which can authentically be made on any of the Outer Hebrides).

Hushinish

From Old Norse *hús* (house) and *i nes* (at the headland) with a bit of Gaelic softening of the s sounds.

Knock

Gaelic *cnoc* means hill. Although the Gaelic is pronounced crock, the modern English name has anglicized the spelling, oddly ignoring the pronunciation.

Laxay

From Old Norse *lax* (salmon) and the very short Old Norse word *á* which means river.

Lewis

The tortuous naming history of Harris' low-lying northern neighbour is thought to originate with Old Norse *lýðr* (people, common folk) – or its plural form *lýðir* – together with *hús* (home); then down via Gaelic *leòdhas* [l-yoh-uhs].

Manish

This is likely to be from Old Norse *már* (seagull) and *nes* (headland).

Minch, The

This is thought to be Old Norse in origin: *megin* (main) and *nes* (headland). A Gaelic softening of the s in *nes* would take this closer in sound to Minch, although Gaels have totally different names for this stretch of water.

Obbe

From Gaelic *òb* (bay).

> *Obbe is now called Leverburgh after the philanthropist Lord Leverhulme, who, in the early 20th century, started the replacement of the old black houses with more modern buildings. Its Gaelic name is still An t-Ob (the bay).*

Pabbay

Quite likely to be from Old Norse *papa* (Irish monk) and *ey* (island).

Rodel

From Old Norse *rá* (roe deer) and *dalr* (valley).

Scalpay

The –ay is from Old Norse *ey* (island) and the Scalp– is very probably linked to the naming background of Scapa Flow in Orkney as meaning shellfish.

Scarp

This might be named after Old Norse *skarfr* (cormorant) or after Gaelic *sgarbh* [skarf] which also means cormorant. But another possibility is Old Norse *skárpr* meaning barren, which does seem a likelier reason for giving a name.

Seaforth, Loch

From Old Norse *sær* (sea, salt lake) plus *fjǫrðr* (fjord). Loch of the salty fjord.

Shader

An Old Norse *sætr* was a homestead
or farm and Shader is possibly an
anglicized form of this, via the Gaelic
name Siadar [shee-uhtuhr].

> *The Steinacleit Cairn and
> Stone Circle are thought
> to be the remains of a
> prehistoric farm at Shader.*

Shawbost

The –bost is a commonly found element contracted from Old Norse
bólstaðr (farm, homestead) and the Shaw– is likely to come from Old
Norse *sjá* (sea loch).

Stornoway

There are two less than totally satisfactory possibilities for the
derivation of the name of the main town on Lewis. Either it could be
from Old Norse *stjórn* (steering) and *vágr* (bay). Or from Old Norse
stjarna (star) plus *vágr*.

Taransay

The island or, in Old Norse, *ey* of a man called Taran or the island
named in honour of Taran.

Tarbert (Harris)

From Gaelic *tairbeart* [teruh-buhrsht] (isthmus, portage point).
What's that? Portage points were important places in days when
goods off a boat, or the whole boat itself, had to be dragged up the
shore and overland to the next loch or stretch of sea.

Uig

This is a Gaelicized form of the Old Norse *vík* (bay). There's also a Uig
Bay, a typical example of the original name, which had a meaning to
those that spoke the language, losing its meaning to later inhabitants,
who then called it the same thing in another language.

Valtos

From, it is said, Old Norse *vatnlauss* (waterless).

Northern Highlands ~West

The Old Man of Storr

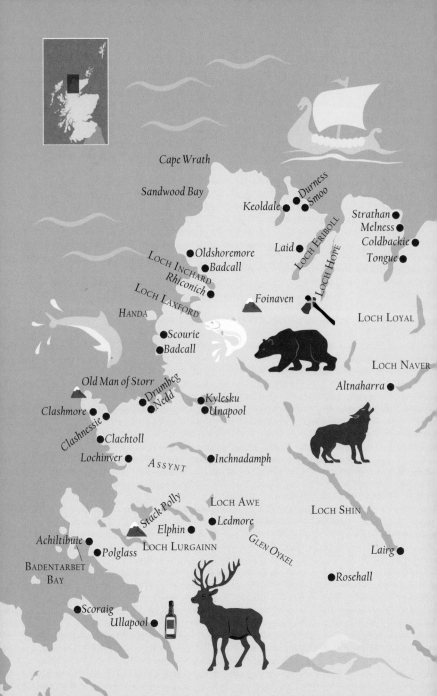

Achiltibuie

There are two schools of thought. A traditional account has the name coming from Gaelic *achadh* [ahK-uhG] (field) and *gille* [geel-yuh] (boy) and *bhuidhe* [voo-yuh] (yellow-haired). Another theory prefers Gaelic *achadh* (field) plus *allt* (stream) plus *buidhe* [boo-yuh] (yellow). Yellow, clayey streams seem a much more likely explanation than yellow-haired boys. Especially if the Gaelic is changed to include a genitive as in *an uillt bhuidhe* [uhn oo-iltch voo-yuh] (of the yellow stream).

Altnaharra

From Gaelic *allt* (stream), *na* (of the) and *eirbhe* [airuh-vuh] (old Gaelic: wall). An *allt* is a stream with steep banks.

Assynt

The name of this district is thought to stem from Old Norse *áss* (rocky ridge). There are two Gaelic names: Asainte [assin-chuh] and Asainn [asseen]. These are just Gaelic versions of the Norse, one of which omits the final –t, which found its way into the English name. It is likely that the –een or –ynt can be accounted for as just the Old Norse definite article –inn, Old Norse definite articles being added to the end of words. So this remote and rugged area is well named as The Rocky Ridge.

Awe, Loch

From old Gaelic *àbh* [ahv] which simply means water. (The bigger and much better known Loch Awe is down in Argyll.)

Badcall

Nothing to do with gambling or decision-making. This means patch of hazel trees from the Gaelic *bad* (place, patch) and old Gaelic *coll* (hazel tree). It's a popular name; there is more than one Badcall up here.

Badentarbet Bay

Sounds a bit Germanic, but it's from Gaelic *bad* (thicket) with *an tairbeirt* [uhn teruh-buhrsht] (at the isthmus).

Cape Wrath

Nothing to do with anger or storms. Wrath is from Old Norse *hverfa* meaning to turn. This is the point at which the Viking ships beating in from the east turned south to descend on the west coast of Scotland.

Clachtoll

From Gaelic *clach* (stone) and *toll* (pit, hole).

Clashmore

Sounds like it should be the site of a big battle. But no, this is from Gaelic *clais* [clash] meaning ditch or trench or furrow and *mòr* meaning big.

Clashnessie

A monster-free zone. Clash is from Gaelic *clais* [clash] which means trench or ditch and old Gaelic *an easaidh* [an essee] (by the little waterfall).

Coldbackie

This is from Old Norse *bakki* (bank) preceded by, most probably, *kol* (charcoal). A charcoal-fired furnace was the best way of forging metals. This would have been a place of some importance in ancient times.

Drumbeg

From Gaelic *druim* [droo-im] (ridge) and *beag* [bek] (little).

Durness

From Old Norse *dýr* (deer) and *nes* (headland).

Elphin

This is from the old Gaelic word *ailbhinn* [eluhvin] which means rocky peak or precipice.

Eriboll, Loch

From Old Norse *eyrr* (spit of land) and *ból* (farm).

Foinaven [pronounced fon-ayven]

From the Gaelic *foinne* [fon-yuh] (wart) together with *bheinn* [vayn] (mountain).

Handa

This is likely to be from Old Norse *sandr* (sand) and *ey* (island). But Gaelic has intervened with its own name *Eilean Shannda*, in which the S is not pronounced, and so the English name follows the Gaelic pronunciation, giving us Handa.

Hope, Loch

It's not a question of hoping. The name comes from Old Norse *hóp* (bay).

Dun Dornaigil Broch stands 5 miles south of the southern end of Loch Hope.

Inchard, Loch

This is thought to come from Old Norse *engi* (meadow, pasture) and *fjǫrðr* (fjord).

Inchnadamph

From Gaelic *innis* [eensh] (riverside meadow) and *nan damh* [nuhn daf] (of the stags).

Keoldale

From Gaelic *cill* (church, holy man's cell) and Old Norse *dalr* (valley, dale).

Kylesku

From Gaelic *caolas* [kurluhs] (straits) and *cumhang* [koo-ang] (narrow).

Laid

This is a curious anglicization of the Gaelic word *leathad* [leh-uht] which means simply slope.

Lairg

From old Gaelic *làirig* [lah-rig] (pass).

Laxford, Loch

From Old Norse *lax* (salmon) and *fjǫrðr* (fjord). The j has gone missing to make it sound less Nordic. There's no ford.

Ledmore

From Gaelic *leathad* [leh-uht] (slope) and *mòr* (big).

Lochinver

The loch at the river mouth, from Gaelic *inbhir* [in-yuhr].

Loyal, Loch

Contracted and anglicized from Old Norse *lǫg* (law) and *fjall* (hill). The loch is named after the hill, which was used as an assembly place for judicial matters.

Lurgainn, Loch

From the Gaelic *lurgann* meaning shin. The Gaelic also means an unshapely leg.

Melness

This is a combination of two quite frequently found Old Norse words: *melr* (grassy sand dune) together with *nes* (headland).

Naver, Loch

In AD150 Ptolemy, in his Geography, has this as Nabaros. The *–ar* is a common Celtic ending for a river name. *Nabh* can be cloud, but this is all theory...

Nedd

From Gaelic *nead* (nest).

Old Man of Storr

The *Stórr* is Old Norse (the Great One). The Gaelic name is Bodach an Stòrr, *bodach* being an old man. But this Gaelic is in fact a euphemism for *Bod an Stòrr* (the penis of Storr), the English translation of the name side-stepping the euphemism.

Oldshoremore

Old Gaelic *àisir* [ahsh-uhr] (path, pass) with the adjective *mòr* (big), strangely expanded into something that sounds vaguely similar in English. There's a Little Oldshore (Oldshore Beg) not far away.

Oykell, Glen

This is likely to be from Brittonic *uchel* which simply means high.

Polglass

From Gaelic *poll* (pool) and *glas* [glash] (grey-green).

Rhiconich

From Gaelic *ruighe* [roo-yuh] which means forearm or, in placenames, slope or lower slope. Gaelic *chòinnich* means mossy.

Rosehall

This sounds very English, too English to be true, given the location. The rose is not a rose but will stem from the Gaelic word *ros*. And this Gaelic word *ros* has several meanings. Here it is likely to mean a wooded area. And the –hall is a fairly standard anglicization of the Scots word *haugh* meaning a riverside meadow.

Sandwood Bay

A strange contortion. The name is thought to originate from Old Norse *sandvatn* meaning sand water.

> *The mile-long beach at Sandwood Bay is held to be the most beautiful beach in the British Isles, discovered and named by Viking adventurers, now only accessible to those prepared to make the 4-mile trek from the nearest road.*

Scoraig

From Old Norse *sguvr* (gully) and a time-warped variant of *vík* to *uig* for the ending –*aig* meaning bay.

> *Scoraig is the remotest of the remote. Nae road.*

Scourie

Possibly from Old Norse *skógr* (wood).

Shin, Loch

From a pre-Celtic word *sinn* (flowing water). In Gaelic this would be pronounced *shin*.

> *The River Shin is a fast-flowing river with falls and a famous salmon leap.*

Smoo

From Old Norse *smuga* (narrow opening, hence hiding place).

> *Smoo is known for its cave and its waterfall.*

Stack Polly

From the Gaelic *stac* (steep rock, stack) and *pollaidh* [polee] (of a pool).

Strathan

The name is from the Gaelic *srath* [stra] together with the diminutive ending *–an*, making this a little valley, although a strath is a flattish river valley and not the usually imagined steep-sided valley.

Tongue

Yes, it does mean tongue, as in tongue of land. Originally from Old Norse *tunga*.

Ullapool

Plenty of water there, but the name doesn't refer to a pool. It's from Old Norse *Olaf*, the personal name, and *ból*, a shortened form of *bólstaðr* (homestead or farm).

Unapool

From Old Norse *Uni*, a person's name, and *ból*, short for *bólstaðr* (homestead or farm).

Northern Highlands
~ East

Whaligoe Steps

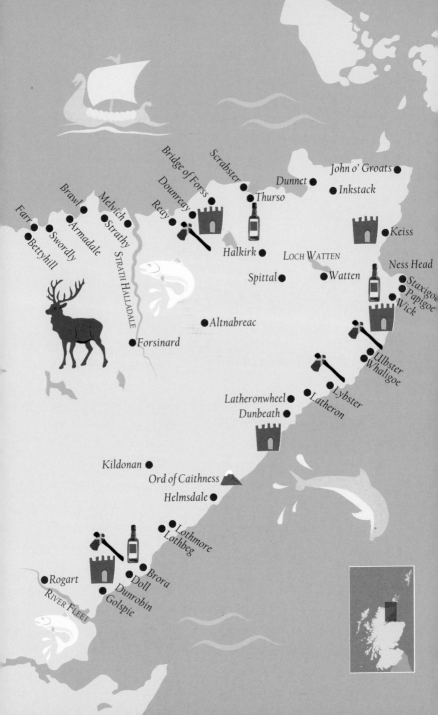

Altnabreac [pronounced altna-brake]

From Gaelic *allt* (stream) and *na breac* [brek] (of the trout).

Armadale

From Old Norse *armr* (arm) and *dalr* (dale). Was it perhaps the shape of the dale that gave rise to this name?

Bettyhill

The name is in honour of the Countess of Sutherland who set up this little place around 1820. She did this to give houses and work to some of those who had suffered so badly in the Highland Clearances.

Brawl

The Vikings did pass along this coast more than once. It is suggested that this name may derive from Old Norse *breiðr hallr* which means broad hillside, appropriate enough topographically. And a later Gaelicization of the pronunciation would see the dropping of the –th– sound (in the Old Norse ð).

Bridge of Forss

From Old Norse *fors* (waterfall).

Brora

From Old Norse *brú* (bridge) and *á* (river, water). So: Bridgewater.

Doll

In old Gaelic a *dol* is a meadow.

Near Doll there's an Iron-Age broch called Carn Liath, a mile south along the main road.

Dounreay

From Gaelic *dùn* [doon] (hill fort) and *ràth* [ra] (circular fort).

Dounreay is the site of a nuclear power station, now being decommissioned, and has as neighbours two Neolithic burial cairns, just to the southeast.

Dunbeath

From the Gaelic *dùn* meaning hill fort and *beithe* [beh-uh] meaning birch tree.

Dunnet

Possibly from Gaelic *dùn* [doon] (hill fort) and *aite* [aht-chuh] (place).

> *Nearby Dunnet Head is the actual northernmost point of the British Isles (mainland).*

Dunrobin

From Gaelic *dùn* [doon] (fort) and Robin, the name of the third Earl of Sutherland.

Farr

Probably from Gaelic *for* (upper). So: High Ground.

Fleet, River

From Old Norse *fljót* (river).

Forsinard

From Old Norse *fors* (waterfall) and Gaelic *na àird* [arsht] (of the heights). So: Upper Falls.

Golspie

From an Old Norse name *Gulli* together with *bú* (farm).

Halkirk

This is possibly from the Old Norse *hár* (high) togther with *kirkja* (church).

Helmsdale

Hjalmund is an Old Norse personal name and this dale is his dale.

Inkstack

Strange name. Could be from a Norse personal name *Inga* and the Gaelic *stac* (projecting rock, hillock). It's all pretty flat around here, so any bump would be a feature.

John o' Groats

Named after a Dutchman, John de Groot, who lived here in the 15th century. Dunnet Head is further north.

Kildonan

This is the *cill* of St Donnan. A *cill* in Gaelic is a church or, more minimally, a holy man's cell.

> *St Donnan was a Celtic evangelizing priest, believed to have been killed in the year 617. Another place that bears his name is the famous castle at Eilean Donan.*

Keiss [pronounced to rhyme with piece]

From Norse *keisa* (to jut out), as nearby Tang Head indeed does, into the North Sea.

Latheron

A very peculiarly contorted name of Gaelic origin in an area where the placenames are predominantly Norse, this is thought to stem from what in more modern Gaelic is *làthach* [lah-oK] (sludge, muddy place). A 13th century record has it as Lagheryn, which helps account for the existence, but not the sense, of the –ron ending, although the whole name has undergone radical anglicization.

Latheronwheel

The Latheron– is the same as described under Latheron above. But the role of anglicization in the recording of placenames reaches a high point of oddity here. The ending –wheel has no connection with any meaning in English or Gaelic. It comes from the Gaelic *a' phuill* [uh foo-eel] (by the pool). So this was a muddy place by the pool.

Lothbeg

I'm loath to say this is old Gaelic *loth* [loh] meaning marsh or mire. And the –beg is from (modern) Gaelic *beag* (little).

Lothmore

Just up the road from Little Mire is Big Mire. Old Gaelic *loth* [loh] (mire) followed by (modern) Gaelic *mòr* (big).

Lybster

This could be from Old Norse *hlif* (shelter, protection) and the typically trimmed-down form of *bólstaðr* (homestead, farm). Or perhaps from the Old Norse word *hlíð* (slope) plus –ster from *bólstaðr*.

> The Neolithic burial chambers, the Grey Cairns of Camster, are 6 miles north of Lybster.

> The Hill o' Many Stanes, 4 miles up the coast from Lybster, is dated at some 3000 years BC. Some 200 stone slabs lie arranged on the hillside. Purpose unknown.

Melvich

From Old Norse *melr* (grassy dune) and *vík* (bay). Well, it still matches this description.

Ness Head

Old Norse *nes* means headland or head. So this is Headland Head or Head Head.

Ord of Caithness

Òrd is old Gaelic for a rounded hill.

Papigoe

The priest's geo. From Old Norse *papa* (priest, monk). A geo is a small fjord, creek or gully off the sea with steep cliffs on either side.

Reay

From Gaelic *ràth* [ra] (circular fort).

Rogart

Thought by some to be from Old Norse *rauðr* (red) and *garðr* (enclosure). But what is a red field? Maybe Old Norse *rá* (roe deer) is a more likely starting point.

Scrabster

The ending –ster is a common contraction of Old Norse *bólstaðr* (farm, homestead). The Scrab– remains a mystery. In the Orkneyinga Saga, written in 1225, it is called Skarabólstaðr. Possibly a Norseman's name.

Spittal

Not as nasty as it sounds. From the old Gaelic *spideal* [spijuhl] meaning refuge or spital.

Staxigoe

The geo of the stack or Gaelic *stac* (big projecting rock). A geo is a small fjord, creek or gully off the sea with steep cliffs on either side.

Strath Halladale

The Halladale, which is also the name of the river, is possibly from Old Norse *helgad dalr* meaning hallowed valley. The addition of the (originally Gaelic) Strath simply repeats the –dalr in another language.

Strathy

From Gaelic *srath* [stra] (flat river valley) and the ending –*aidh* [ee]. So: valley place.

Swordly

Nothing to do with battles or clan warfare. This means simply grassy slope, the sword being from Old Norse *svarð*, a cognate of English sward as in grassy sward.

Thurso

It is thought that the colonizing Vikings named or renamed this place to celebrate one of their gods, giving it more or less its present form: *Þors á* (Thor's river).

Ulbster

From Old Norse, the farm or *bólstaðr* belonging to a man called Ulf.

A Neolithic burial site at Cairn o'Get lies a mile and a half southwest of Ulbster.

Watten

From Old Norse *vatn* meaning simply water or lake.

Watten, Loch

Vatn is Old Norse for water or lake. A no-nonsense name, this Loch Water.

Whaligoe

The –goe ending, common along this stretch of coast, is from Old Norse *gjá* which has generated both Gaelic *geodha* and the specialist English term *geo*, which is a small fjord, creek or gully off the sea with steep cliffs on either side. Whaligoe is the geo of whales.

> *The Whaligoe steps, 330 of them (though when first built there were more), take you down a precipitous path to the harbour hidden at the foot of the cliffs.*

Wick

From Old Norse *vík* meaning bay. There is also Wick Bay, which is really Bay Bay.

> *Old Pulteney is distilled at Wick.*

Outer Hebrides ~ South

Berneray West Beach

BERNERAY

● Otternish

NORTH UIST

● Lochmaddy

● Carinish

GRIMSAY

BENBECULA

● Liniclete

● Iochdar

● Howmore

SOUTH UIST

Daliburgh ●

● Lochboisdale

ERISKAY

Borve ●   BARRA
Castlebay ●
VATERSAY

MINGULAY

BERNERAY

Barra

The Irish missionary St Barr, who died in the early 7th century and who trained evangelists to go out among the heathen Scots and Picts, may well have given his name to this island.

Benbecula

[pronounced with the stress on the BEC]

The Gaelic name is Beinn na Faoghla [bayn nuh vuhla] which is: mountain of the ford. Before the construction of the causeways at the north and south ends of this island, Benbecula was only accessible by wading across the fords or what the Norsemen called *vaðlar*. The island's name has caused a lot of discussion.

> *It was here on Benbecula in 1746 that Bonnie Prince Charlie, on the run from English Redcoats, was looked after by Lady Clanranald and Flora MacDonald, taken to Lady Clanranald's house at Nunton and given woman's clothes which he wore, disguised as one Betty Burke, rowing and sailing over the seas to Skye.*

Although it starts off with a nice clear Ben–, some say that this was originally Gaelic *peighinn* [peh-eenyuh] – land that was farmed for a penny's rent – and that Gaelic *beinn* [bayn] (mountain) is unlikely to have been the original name since the highest point here is no more than some 124 metres above sea level. But against this it should be said that all heights are relative and there are places on this flattish island called *Àird* (height) and *Uachdar* (upper land).

Neither the modern Gaelic name nor the explanation via pennylands go far toward throwing light on the origins. It is significant that the stress in the English name is on the second syllable, the BEC and these explanations sidestep that.

The historical names are a mix. Recorded forms are Beanbeacla (1495), Benbicula (1660); in between in the 16th century there is Benvalgha and Buchalga.

If we put the Gaelic *beag* [bek] (little) back in – although in modern Gaelic it would here be *bheag* [vek] – we come to Beinn b(h)eag na Faoghla [bayn b/vek nuh vuhla], the little mountain of the fords.

It is imaginable how English-speaking scribes would have recorded as best they could what they heard from a variety of Gaels. What the Old Norse called the island, that is not known.

Berneray

Old Norse Bjorn's *ey* (island). There are two Bernerays shown on the map.

Borve

From Old Norse *borg* (fort).

Carinish

The Gaelicized *nes* or headland of the Norseman called Kari.

Castlebay

Just what it says on the signs.

> *Kisimul Castle can be reached by boat from Castlebay.*

Daliburgh

From Old Norse *dalr* (valley) and *borg* (fort).

Eriskay

The Norseman Eric's *ey* or island.

Grimsay

The *ey* or island of the Old Norseman called Grim.

Hebrides

Neither Gaels nor Norsemen are behind this name. The Gaels call the Inner Hebrides Na h-Eileanan A-Staigh (the Inner Islands) and the Outer Hebrides Na h-Eileanan A-Muigh (the Outer Islands) and the Hebrides as a whole Na h-Eileanan Siar (the Western Isles) or Innse Gall (the Islands of the Strangers), those strangers being Norse. And the Norsemen themselves called the Hebrides Suðreyjar (southern islands). The English name pre-dates those in origin and comes down via the Roman scholar and commander, Pliny the Elder, who recorded the islands as Hebudae, then later via Ptolemy with Ebudae, with someone many years along the way mistaking a handwritten u for ri, bequeathing the name to us thus (without any allocation of meaning).

Celtic Cross at Howmore

Howmore

Probably from Old Norse *haugr* (mound) and Gaelic *mòr* (big). The Gaelic name is Tobha Mòr [toh-wuh mor] or Togh Mòr [toh mor] neither of which have any connection with mound, *tobha* meaning rope.

Iochdar

The Gaelic word *ìochdar* [ee-uhK-kuhr] means bottom, as in low-lying ground.

Liniclete

Its Gaelic name is Lìonacleit [lee-uhnuh-klech] and the derivation can be traced along several interrelated threads: from Old Norse *klettr* (rocks, cliff) and the word *lin* which means flax in Old Norse and also in Gaelic *lìon* [lee-uhn]. And Gaelic *cleite* [klay-chuh] is a rocky outcrop.

Lochboisdale

From Gaelic *loch* put in front of derived forms of Old Norse *bug* (bay) and *dalr* (valley). So: valley bay loch, loch bay valley, whichever you like. There is no loch called Boisdale.

Lochmaddy

Dog loch. From Gaelic *nam mhadaidh* [nuhm vatee] (of the dog).

Mingulay

The name is thought to come from Old Norse *mikkil* (big) with *ey* (island).

North Uist

Some say Uist is from Old Norse *i-vist* (in dwelling). But a connection with Old Norse *vestr* (the west, in the west) is also plausible.

Otternish

Not otters but sandbars. From Gaelic *oitir* [otchir] (sandbar or reef) plus –nish from Old Norse *nes* (headland or spit).

South Uist

see North Uist

Vatersay

Some say this is water island from Old Norse *vatn* (water) and *ey* (island). A strange Norse choice though. Why would the Norsemen call it that? Another possibility is Old Norse *vatr* (wet).

The remnants of an Iron-Age broch can be seen on Vatersay.

Skye

The Black Cuillins

Achnacloich

From Gaelic *achadh* [ahK-uhG] (field) and *na cloich* [nuh-kloyK] (of the stone). So: Stonefield.

Armadale

This could be from Old Norse *armr* (arm) and *dalr* (dale, valley).

Borrodale

From Old Norse *borg* (fort) and *dalr* (valley). So: valley of the fort.

Bracadale

From Old Norse *brekka* (slope) and *dalr* (valley).

Braes, The

Just the Scots word for hills, which, in its turn, comes from the Gaelic *bràigh* [brY] (upland).

Brittle, Glen

Nothing brittle about it, it's from Old Norse *breiðr* (broad) and *vík* (bay), the glen being named after the bay.

Broadford

Just what it says, the broad ford. The Gaelic name for this town is An t-àth Leathann [uhn tah-leh-huhn] (the broad ford). Unusually here, the literal English translation has stuck.

Carbost

There's more than one Carbost on Skye. The second syllable of the name comes from Old Norse *bólstaðr* (farm). The first element may well be from the farm owner's name.

> *Dun Ardtreck is an Iron-Age broch northwest of the more westerly Carbost.*

Clachan

From Gaelic *clachan* (stones). Were the houses here notable for being built of stone? Or was it a good place to quarry stones? *Clachan* in Gaelic also means hamlet and, in older Gaelic, church graveyard.

Coruisk, Loch

From Gaelic *coire* (corrie) and *uisge* [oosh-guh] (water).

Cuillins

One possibility is that this elusive mountain name stems from Old Norse *kjǫlr*, which has the basic meaning of a keel, and then, as a secondary figurative sense from that, of a keel-shaped range of mountains. Add the Norse ending which is equivalent to the definite article 'the' and you have *kjǫlrinn*. There are Cuillins on the Island of Rum too, likewise keel-shaped.

Digg

A haven for archeologists? Gaelic *dig* is a ditch.

Dunvegan

From Gaelic *dùn* [doon] (fort) and an Old Norse person's name, *Began*.

Edinbane

From Gaelic *aodann* [uh-dahn] (face, as in hill face) and *bàn* [bahn] (white).

Eishort, Loch

It is thought that this may be from Old Norse *eið* (isthmus) and *fjǫrðr* (fjord).

Flashader

The Fla– is probably from Old Norse *flatr* (flat). An Old Norse *setr* was a homestead or farm and –shader occurs as a Gaelicized form of this.

Greepe

The Gaelic *grìob* [greep] means rocky shore.

Heribusta

A nice Old Norse remnant, meaning the Lord's farm (not God's). From the *bólstaðr* (farm) of the *herra* (lord).

Kilbeg

From Gaelic *cill* (church) and *beag* (little): Littlechurch.

Kilmore

From Gaelic *cill* (church) and *mòr* (big): Bigchurch.

Kilmuir

From Gaelic *cill* (church) and *Mhuire* [vooruh] which is an older Gaelic form of *Mhoire* (of Mary).

Kyleakin

From Gaelic *caol* [kurl] (straits) and Old Norse *Haakon* (the name of a king of Norway).

> *Imagine a fleet of Viking longships anchored off Kyleakin, the year 1263, King Haakon preparing to sail down the western coast, the expedition to end with failure at the Battle of Largs.*

Luib

From Gaelic *lùb* which simply means bend.

Peinlich

One for the German speakers? No, of course it's not German *peinlich* – which means painful or embarrassing. This name, it is said, stems from Gaelic *peighinn an lighiche* [peh-een-yuh uhn lee-eeKuh]. This is the doctor's pennyland, that is to say land which was rented for the sum of one penny (a custom which has elsewhere generated the name prefix Pin–).

Portree

This is from Gaelic *port* (port) and *ruighe* [roo-yuh] which means forearm but, in placenames, slope or lower slope. Which plainly describes the site. The modern Gaelic name is Port Rìgh [porsht ree-yuh], which means King's Harbour, the name having been changed or re-interpreted, possibly after a visit by King James V.

> *The Battle of the Braes took place near Portree in the year 1882, when local crofters took up arms to oppose unfair grazing rights. 50 policemen were shipped in from Glasgow, backed up soon after by the marines. The uprising did finally lead to land reform under Gladstone's government.*

Raasay

From Old Norse *rár* (roe deer) and *ey* (island). Some think there was also Old Norse *áss* (ridge) after the *rár*.

Scavaig, Loch

The –vaig is probably Old Norse *vík* (bay). Sca– might be from an ancient river name.

Skye

Perhaps connected with Gaelic *sgiathach* [skee-uh-hoK] which means winged. In AD150 the island was referred to by Ptolemy as Ski or Skitis or Scetis.

Sleat [pronounced slate]

Old Norse *sléttr* means level; and *sletta* is a level field.

Sligachan

From Gaelic *sligeach* [shlig-uhK] (shelly) and the diminutive ending *–an*. So: Little Shelly Place.

Snizort, Loch

This might well be connected with the Old Norse verb *sníða* (to cut) plus *fjǫrðr* (fjord), since the loch here is cut or split into several stretches.

Soay

This is from Old Norse *sauðr* (sheep) and *ey* (island).

Staffin

This is probably connected with Old Norse *stafr* (rod, pillar) as the rock formations on Staffin Island will testify. (The –in ending matches up with the Old Norse equivalent for 'the'.)

Struan

From Gaelic *sruth* [stroo] (stream) and the ending *–an*, meaning little or –let.

> *Dun Beag, an Iron-Age broch just northwest of Struan, with its still clearly massive walls, was probably constructed around 200 BC. Dun Beag is Gaelic for small fort. Clearly these old Gaels enjoyed a little dry understatement.*

Talisker

This name is thought to be from Old Norse *hallr* (sloping) and *sker* (rock). No shortage of these in Scotland. But where's the T in the name? If the Norse were Gaelicized this would become An t-'hallr sker' (the sloping rock), with the t sound replacing the h.

Tarskavaig

This is thought to be from Old Norse *þorskr* (cod) and *vík* (bay).

Teangue

From Gaelic *teanga* (tongue, spit of land).

Tote

There's more than one Tote on Skye and the name comes, with some anglicizing, from Old Norse *toft* or *topt*, which is either a homestead or a site where building work is going on or has been going on.

Near the Tote which is just northwest of Portree you can see a Pictish stone known as Clach Ard (Gaelic for tall stone). This is a rarity in the west of Scotland, most Pictish stones being away in the east.

Uig

This is a Gaelicized form of the Old Norse *vík* (bay). There's also a Uig Bay (which is to say Bay Bay, a nice example of how meaningful descriptive reference becomes just meaningless name when the local language changes).

Valtos

This could be from Old Norse *vatnlauss* which means waterless.

Central Highlands
~ West

Glen Affric

Achanalt

From Gaelic *achadh* [ahK-uhG] (field) plus *nan allt* (of the streams).

Achnasheen

From Gaelic *achadh* [ahK-uhG] (field), *na sìne* [nuh shee-nuh] (of the storm).

Achnashellach

From Gaelic *achadh* [ahK-uhG] (field), *nan seileach* [nuhn sheluhK] (of the willows).

Affric, Glen/Loch/River

From Gaelic *àth* [ah] (ford) and then *bhraich* [vrYK], a wild beast of uncertain species variously defined in dictionaries of older Gaelic as boar, bear, dog, stag and badger.

> *Glen Affric is well known as the district where much of the original and typical ancient Caledonian forest is still to be found. This is an area of exceptional scenic beauty.*

Alsh, Loch

Perhaps from Gaelic *aillse* [Yl-shuh] (fairy). Rejected by some as a derivation. But then the old Gaels did tell stories about water spirits.

Applecross

Don't go looking for apple trees. The *apple* comes from Brittonic *aber*, which means river mouth. And the river here was known as Crosan. *Aber* is rarely found in place names in the Western Highlands.

Badachro

It was thought that this came from Gaelic *bad* (thicket) and *chròch* [KrohK] (saffron), saffron being an important dye. But this naming theory has been challenged by Gaelic *Bad a' Chrò* (thicket by the fold), the fold being for livestock.

Badcaul, Badicaul

This means patch of hazel trees from the Gaelic *bad* (place, patch) and old Gaelic *coll* (hazel tree). A popular name.

Balmacara

From Gaelic *baile* [baluh] (homestead, place) and *Macara* (which is a clan).

Braemore

From Gaelic *bràigh* [brY] (upland) and *mòr* (big).

Broom, Loch

Probably not the flower that blossoms on the banks, this comes from Gaelic *braon* [brurn] which means something like falling water or drizzle. The loch higher up has the Gaelic name Loch a' Bhraoin [vrurn].

Carron, Loch

This is thought to be from an early Celtic root form *kar* (rough) and the ending *–on* used to denote water.

Cove

Easy. But it's not the English word meaning bay. Old Norse *kofi* means hut. There are several Coves in Scotland.

Diabaig, Loch

This is thought to be from Old Norse *djúp* (deep) and *vík* (bay).

Dornie

Gaelic *dòirneag* [dornak] is a pebble.

Drumbuie

From Gaelic *druim* [droo-im] (ridge) and *buidhe* [boo-yuh] (yellow).

Duich, Loch

This is a loch named after St Duthach whose name in Gaelic is pronounced [doo-uhK]. St Duthach was a much venerated holy man who died in the year 1065.

Eilean Donan

From Gaelic *eilean* [aylan] (island) and the personal name *Donnan*.

St Donnan, honoured by the island named after him, was a Celtic priest, whose mission was to bring the Christian religion to the Picts. He was killed in AD 617.

Ewe, Loch

Not sheep, it's from old Gaelic *iù* [yew] (yew tree). Did some scribe not like Loch Yew?

Fada, Loch

Fada being Gaelic for long, which this loch once was by local standards.

Fada, Lochan

A *lochan* is a little loch and *fada* means long in Gaelic. A long little loch.

Gairloch

From Gaelic *geàrr* [g-yahr] (short).

Garry, Loch

The old Celtic word *gar* means rough. So does Gaelic *garbh* [garav].

Glenelg

From Gaelic *gleann* [gl-yown] (glen) and *ealg* [eluhg] an old Gaelic word for noble. It is also possible that the elg element comes from *Eilg*, an old Gaelic name for Ireland.

> There are two well-preserved Iron-Age brochs near Glenelg.

Glomach, Falls of

From old Gaelic *glòm* (chasm) and the ending *–ach* (place of).

> At 113m or 370 feet The Falls of Glomach are Britain's highest waterfall but can only be reached if you're up for a 5 hour trek there and back.

Hourn, Loch

From Gaelic *sòrn* (kiln, although these days the word refers to the flue of the kiln). But why has the s changed to h? Well, the Gaelic name goes through what is called a process of lenition and slenderization so that Loch *sòrn* becomes Loch Shuirn. And in that Gaelic name the s is not pronounced. The English name follows the spoken Gaelic form.

Inverewe

From Gaelic *inbhir* [in-yuhr] (mouth) and *Ewe* (the river's name), which is from old Gaelic *iù* [yew] (yew tree) which has been given sheep's clothing.

> *Inverewe is famous for its lush tropical gardens. If you're looking for it on the map, go to Poolewe.*

Keppoch

From Gaelic *ceap* [k-yep] (top) and the ending *–ach* (field).

Kinlochewe

From Gaelic *ceann* [k-yown] (head) and Loch Ewe. But wrong loch surely? It's at the head of Loch Maree. Well, up to the middle of the 17th century Loch Maree was called Loch Ewe. The village itself didn't get a name change as did the loch.

Kintail

From Gaelic *ceann* [k-yown] (head) and *an t-sàile* [uhn taluh] (of the salt-water).

Kishorn

From Norse *keisa* (to jut out) and *horn* (cape, horn).

Knoydart

From the Old Norse name *Cnut* and *fjǫrðr* (fjord), down through Gaelic, in which it is called Cnoideart [kroy-dehrsht]. But the anglicized pronunciation has prevailed.

Kyle of Lochalsh

From Gaelic *caol* [kurl] (straits).

Letterewe

From Gaelic *leitir* [letchir] (hillside). The –ewe is an anglicized rendering of Gaelic *Iù*, which is the name of the river here. *Iù* is old Gaelic for yew tree.

Letters

Nothing postal. From Gaelic *leitir* [letchir] meaning hillside.

Lochcarron

Named after the loch, see Carron

Long, Loch

It's not particularly long by Scottish standards, but then Long doesn't mean long. The name comes from Gaelic *luing* [loo-ing] (of ships), *long* being the nominative singular form. The longer Loch Long, which is a bit better known, is down in Argyll.

Maree, Loch

From the name of the saint Maelrubha. An island in the loch, home to a pre-Christian cult, was called, in Gaelic, Eilean Ma-ruibhe [aylan ma-roo-yuh]. The loch took the name of the cult on the island.

Monar, Loch

Probably from Gaelic *monadh* [monuhG] (hill, moor).

Plockton

From Gaelic *ploc* (clod, as in lump of soil) and the English ending *–ton* (place). The word *ploc* is also attested as a lumpish promontory, of which there are a few around here.

Poolewe

Sheep dip? No. From Gaelic *poll* (pool) and the river name *Ìu*, which is an old Gaelic word for yew tree.

Quoich, Loch

From an older sense of Gaelic *cuach* which becomes, in its genitive form, *cuaich* [koo-eeK] and which means hollow. So: Loch of the Hollow (as they mostly are).

Shiel Bridge

Probably from an old Celtic word *sal* (flowing).

The Jacobite rising known as 'The 19' was put down at the battle of Glenshiel near Shiel Bridge in the year 1719.

Shieldaig

Not shields but fish. This is from Old Norse *síld* (herring) and the *–aig* is a Scotticized or Gaelicized variant of Old Norse *vík* (bay).

Strath

Straightforwardly from Gaelic *srath* [stra], which is a flat river valley.

Stromeferry

Probably from Old Norse *straumr* (current). The ferry is just that.

Torridon, Loch

In the Gaelic it's Toirbheartan [toruh-vershtuhn], a name cognate with Tarbert, which stems from the name of a place where boats could be dragged overland at a narrow isthmus from one loch to another.

Central Highlands
~East

Cromarty Lighthouse

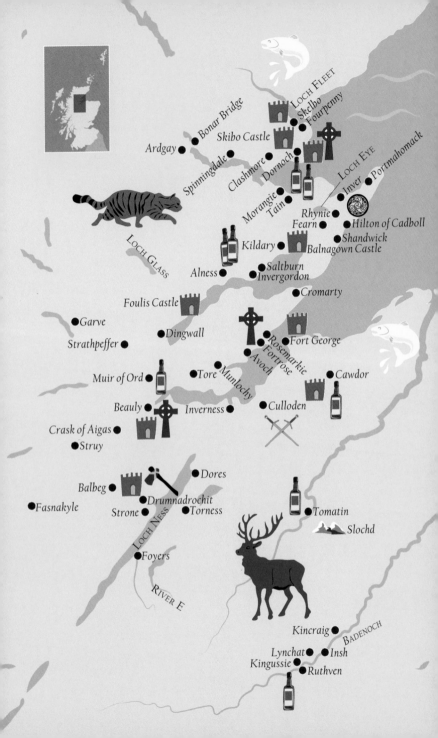

Alness

From Gaelic ending –*ais* [esh] which means something like *place of* added to the name of a local stream, which was probably *alauna* in very early pre-Celtic times.

Ardgay

Windy height, from Gaelic *àrd* (high) or *àirde* [arshtuh] (height, headland) and *gaoithe* [gur-yuh] (of the wind).

Avoch [pronounced awch]

From old Gaelic *àbh* [ahv] (water) with *ach* [ahK] (bank).

Badenoch

From old Gaelic *bàithte* [bah-chuh] (liable to flooding) and the ending for places –*ach*.

Balbeg

From Gaelic *baile beag* [baluh bek] which means small farm or small homestead.

Balnagown Castle

The Gaelic is *baile* [baluh] (home, place) and *nan gobhainn* [nuhn Goh-een] (of the smiths). Variants of Balnagown are common throughout Scotland, blacksmiths being very important people. In this place the smithy was long ago replaced by a castle.

Beauly

From French *beau* [bo] (beautiful) and *lieu* [l-yuh] (place), though with standard mangling of the French pronunciation this has become b-yoo-lee. It's relatively rare for the ancients to reflect their feeling for the beauty of nature in a name. The modern Gaelic name is blunter: A' Mhanachainn [uh vanuhKeen] (the monastery).

Bonar Bridge

Gaelic *bonn* [bown] (bottom) and *àth* [ah] (ford).

Cawdor

From Brittonic *caled* (hard, rapid) and old Gaelic *dobhar* [doh-wuhr] (water).

Macbeth was Thane of Cawdor.

Clashmore

This sounds as though it should be the site of a big battle. But no, this is from Gaelic *clais* [clash] meaning ditch or trench or furrow and *mòr* meaning big. Not a lot of romantic poetry there.

Crask of Aigas

A splendid-sounding name. A Gaelic *crasg* is a crossing place, especially over a ridge. Aigas remains mysterious.

Cromarty

From Gaelic *crom* (crooked) and *àird* [arsht] (height).

Culloden

Very uncertain. It may be from from Gaelic *cùl* [kool] (back) and *lodan* (little pool).

A Bronze Age cemetry (Clava Cairns) can be seen just 300 yards east of the scene of the battle of Culloden.

Culloden is the famous site of the overwhelming defeat of the Scots under Bonnie Prince Charlie in 1746 at the hands of the Duke of Cumberland's savage army.

Dingwall

Nothing to do with walls. The –wall is from Old Norse *vǫllr* (field) and the Ding– from Old Norse *þing* (parliament, assembly). This is a field in which people would come together to discuss and decide local issues and administer justice.

Dores

From the Gaelic *dubh* [doo] (black, dark) and the old Gaelic word *ros* which, among other things, can mean wood.

Dornoch

Gaelic *dòirneag* [dornak] is a pebble. But this place is pebbly no more. The pebbles have turned to sand or have been washed away.

Pop star Madonna got married in the cathedral here at Dornoch. And the last known Scottish execution of a witch took place here in 1722.

Drumnadrochit

From Gaelic *druim* [droo-im] (ridge) and *na drochaid* [droKij] (of the bridge). So: Ridge-by-the-Bridge or maybe Bridge-by-the-Ridge.

Urquhart Castle rises over Loch Ness hard by Drumnadrochit.

There's a Bronze Age chambered cairn at Corrimony, 8 miles west of Drumnadrochit.

E, River [pronounced just like the letter e]

You won't find many names shorter than this. This is thought to be from Old Norse *à* meaning simply river, although the vowel sound has shifted somewhat over the centuries and is probably not how the Norseman said it.

Eye, Loch

Possibly from Old Norse *eið* meaning isthmus.

Fasnakyle

From old Gaelic *fas* (place or, in names, stance) and *na coille* [kuhl-yuh] (of the wood, forest). A stance was where cattle were kept overnight when being driven to market or other pastures.

Fearn

From Gaelic *feàrna* [f-yahrnuh] (alders).

Fleet, Loch

Probably from Old Norse *fljótr* (swift) named after the river. The loch here is tidal.

Fort George

Named after King George II.

> Fort George was built as a garrison for troops dispatched to control the Scottish Highlands after the 1745 Jacobite rebellion.

Fortrose

From Gaelic *fo* (below) and an old sense of Gaelic *ros* (headland).

Foulis Castle [pronounced fowls]

This is thought to be from an old Gaelic term *foghlais* [folish] which is a small stream or a tributary to a larger river.

Fourpenny

Gaelic *peighinn* [peh-een-yuh] is land that was farmed for a penny's rent. The name here is the price the landlord charged.

Foyers

From old Gaelic *fothair* [fohir] meaning terraced hillside.

Garve

From Gaelic *garbh* [garav] (rough).

Glass, Loch

Glas in Gaelic means grey or greyish-green. But this is probably from an older Gaelic sense of *glas* which is water or stream.

Hilton of Cadboll

From Gaelic *cat* (cat) and the first syllable of Old Norse *bólstaðr* (farm).

> The original Cadboll stone is in the National Museum of Scotland in Edinburgh, but there is a replica of this Pictish stone here in Hilton of Cadboll where it was first discovered.

Hilton of Cadboll stone, detail

Insh

From Gaelic *innis* [eensh] which can mean both island and water-meadow.

Inver

From Gaelic *inbhir* [in-yuhr]. Usually a prefix to longer names, *inver* refers to a place where two rivers come together or where a river flows into a loch or the sea.

Invergordon

The name was made up in honour of the 18th century landowner, Sir Alexander Gordon, showing how the Scotticized version of Gaelic *inbhir* [in-yuhr] had become detached from its original reference of river mouth, there being no river mouth here and no river Gordon.

Inverness

From Gaelic *inbhir* [in-yuhr] (mouth) and *nis* (an ancient pre-Celtic river name).

Kildary

From Gaelic *caol* [kurl] (narrow) and *daraidh* [daree] which is an obsolete ending meaning something like 'at the ... place'.

Kincraig

From Gaelic *ceann* [k-yown] (head) and *na creige* [Kreh-kuh] (of the crag).

Kingussie [pronounced kin-yoosee]

Nothing to do with any king. The word break comes after the Kin–. From Gaelic *cinn* (at the head of) and *a' giùthsach* [yoo-saK] (of the pine forest). So: Piney Head.

Kingussie is home to the Speyside Distillery.

Lynchat

This is from old Gaelic *lann* [lown] (enclosure, field) and *chait* [Kaych] (of the cat). A field where wildcats roamed.

Morangie

From Gaelic *mòr* (big) and *innse* [eenshuh] (water meadows).

Muir of Ord

Scots *muir* (moor) and old Gaelic *òrd* (round hill).

Munlochy

The Mun– is probably Gaelic *bun* [boon] (source, origin), and the second part of the name from old Gaelic *lòch* (black, dark) and Irish Gaelic *dae* (goddess), the dark loch here being Munlochy Bay.

Ness, Loch

Well, Old Norse *nes* means headland or cape, but this loch had a name long before the Vikings arrived. Like many other loch or river names, its origins go back into uncharted pre-history.

Portmahomack

From Gaelic *port* (port), *mo* (my) and Irish Gaelic *Cholmáig* which is the name of a Celtic saint, usually rendered in English as Colman.

Rhynie

From Gaelic *ràthan* [rahan] (small circular fort). It was recorded as Rathne in 1529.

Rosemarkie

From old Gaelic *ros* (promontory) and *marc* (horse).

Ruthven [pronounced rivven]

From Gaelic *ruadh* [roo-uhG] (red) and *abhainn* [avin] (river).

Saltburn

Contraband salt was hidden in burns (streams) in the days when there was a tax on salt.

Shandwick

From Old Norse *sandr* (sand) and *vík* (bay). But where did the Sean-Connery-style sh sound come from? Either the Norsemen already pronounced this shand or they pronounced it more like sownd, in which case the Gaels would have had to insert an e (because of the way the Gaelic language works) – giving seownd [sh...]. In this part of Scotland Gaelic has a longer history than Norse, so Gaelic would be calling the shots.

Skelbo

Possibly from Old Norse *skel* (shell) and *ból* (farm); although *sker* has also been put forward, meaning rock.

Skibo Castle

Possibly from old Gaelic *sgiobal* [skipuhl] (granary) or from Old Norse *Skithi* (a personal name) and *ból* (farm).

Slochd

This is an old Gaelic word (the modern term is *sloc*) meaning pit or hollow.

Spinningdale

From Old Norse *spong* (speckle) and *dalr* (dale). The 18th century spinning mill fitted in quite nicely.

Strathpeffer

From Gaelic *srath* [stra] (wide river valley) and an old Brittonic word *pevr* which means a shining or glistening stream.

Strone

From Gaelic *sròn* [stron] which means both nose and point of land.

Struy

From Gaelic *sruth* [stroo] (current, stream) with an ending to denote place: *sruthaigh* [stroo-ee]. So: place of the current.

Tain

A pre-Celtic river name, cognate with Tyne in England. There's another Tain up in Caithness near Thurso. *Tain* is also an old Gaelic word for water.

> *Glenmorangie Distillery is close by Tain.*

Tomatin

From Gaelic *tom* (hillock) and *aiteann* [ay-chuhn] (juniper).

Tore

From Gaelic *todhar* [toh-uhr] (bleaching). The word also means manuring. Both relevant to the way of life.

Torness

Ness is often from Old Norse *nes* (headland), but that is not so likely here. This is very likely to be from Gaelic *tòrr* (hill) and possibly *an easa* (of the waterfall).

Moray

The Lairig Ghru

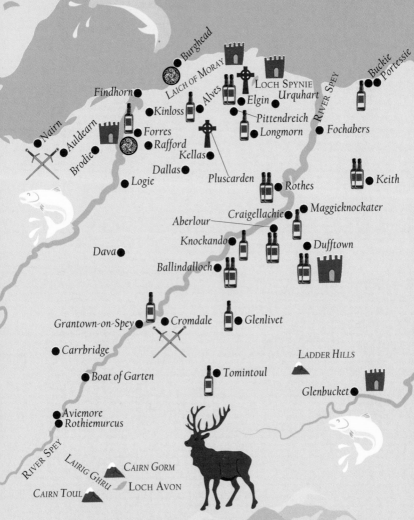

Aberlour

From Brittonic-Pictish *aber* (river mouth) and Gaelic *labhar* [low-uhr] (loud). So: loud place where rivers meet.

Alves

It is thought that this may be from an older Gaelic word *ailbhe* [eluhvuh] (rock) together with a place-indicator ending *–ais* [esh]. So: rocky place.

Auldearn

The name is likely to come from Gaelic *allt* (stream) and *Èireann* (of Ireland).

> *The Battle of Auldearn in 1645 was a victory for the Earl of Montrose's royalist army over the Covenanters.*

Aviemore

From Gaelic *aghaidh* [uh-Gee] (face) and *mhòr* [vor] (big), the face being the mountainside.

Avon, Loch

From the Gaelic *abhainn* [avin] (river). There are, of course, Avons all over Britain, in England much more so than in Scotland.

Ballindalloch

From the Gaelic *baile* [baluh] (homestead, place) and *na dalach* (of the waterside meadow).

Boat of Garten

Just that. There used to be a ferry boat here which plied across the river Garten.

Brodie

From an older Gaelic word *brothag* [broh-hak] (ditch, hollow).

Buckie

A buckie in Scots is a whelk.

Burghead

Although the site is very old, the name is less so, coming from the Old Norse *borg* (fort) with English *head* tacked on, in view of the location on a spit of land.

> This is the site of what is thought to be an ancient Pictish capital, dating back to possibly AD 300. The Burghead Bulls are good examples of Pictish stone carvings. And the Burghead Well is one of Scotland's most mysterious (and spookiest) ancient remains.

Cairn Gorm

From Gaelic *càrn* (hill) and *gorm* [goruhm] (blue). There are several hills with this name in Scotland. This particular one has lent its name to the whole range, the Cairngorms, as well as to the National Park. The Gaels, seeing things their own way, call the Cairngorms the red mountains (am Monadh Ruadh).

Cairn Toul

From Gaelic *càrn* (hill, cairn) and *tuathal* [too-uh-huhl] (ominous, unlucky). Its Gaelic name is Càrn an t-Sabhail [uhn ta-uhl] which means barn hill.

> Cairn Toul is the fourth highest mountain in Scotland.

Carrbridge

A mixture of languages. The Carr– probably comes from older Gaelic *càrr* meaning rocky projection (*càrr* has many other meanings – bog, stag and more).

Craigellachie

The first part of this name is from Gaelic *creag* [krek] (rock). The second part is less clear, but is thought to contain the Gaelic word *eileach*

> The name Craigellachie was the warcry of the Grant clan.

[eluhK] which in modern use is a mill dam, but in older use was a bank of stones or a place with stones where water could be crossed.

Cromdale

From Gaelic *crom* (crooked) and *dail* [dal] (field, meadow).

The Battle of Cromdale in 1690 was a defeat for the Jacobites.

Dallas

From Gaelic *dail* [dal] (field) and *eas* [es] (waterfall).

Dava

From Gaelic *damh* [daf] (ox, stag) and *àth* [ah] (ford). So: Oxford or Stagford.

Dufftown

Named after one James Duff, fourth Earl of Fife, in 1817.

The place is just overflowing with distilleries. As well as Dufftown itself, you have: Balvenie, Glendullan, Glenfiddich, Kininvie and Mortlach.

Elgin

From an old Gaelic name for Ireland *Ealg* [eluhg] with the diminutive ending *−in*. So: Little Ireland. The human habit of nostalgically transferring placenames from country to country goes far back in time. Unless, of course, the locals called it this because of the large number of Irish immigrants.

There's a whole cluster of distilleries here in and around Elgin: Glen Elgin, Glenlossie, Glen Moray, Linkwood, Mannochmore and Miltonduff.

Findhorn

From the Gaelic *fionn* [fewn] (white, fair) and a pre-Celtic river name *erin*, which thought by some to be cognate with river names such as the Rhine or the Rhône.

Fochabers

From Brittonic-Pictish *fothach* (lake) and *aber* (mouth). Well lakes don't have mouths, or do they? Fochabers is near the flood plain of the River Spey.

Forres

It is thought that the name has a connection with old Gaelic *far* (below) and *ras* (shrubs). The name may also have the sense of little woods.

Forres is home to Scotland's tallest Pictish cross-slab, Sueno's Stone.

Glenbucket

Previously Glenbuchat, now tediously and mundanely reduced to an item of household equipment. The Gaelic name is Gleannbuichead which means simply Buichead's Glen.

Glenlivet

From Gaelic *gleann* [gl-yown] (glen) with old Gaelic *liobh* [lee-uhv] (shiny) and *ait* [etch] (place).

Grantown-on-Spey

No mysteries here. The town is named after a local landowner, Sir James Grant.

Keith

From Cumbric or old Gaelic *coit* [kotch] (wood). Related to Welsh *coed* (wood).

Kellas

From Gaelic *ceall* [k-yal] (holy man's cell) and the ending –*ais* [esh], which indicates a place.

Kinloss

From Gaelic *ceann* [k-yown] (head) and *lios* [lis] (garden). Possibly an earlier abbey garden.

Knockando

From Gaelic *cnoc* [krok] (*hill*) and *cheannachd* [K-yanoKk] (trade, commerce). In 1685 the Kk sound at the end was still there, in writing (Knockandoch).

Ladder Hills

The English name is a translation of the Gaelic name for these hills, Monadh an Fhàraidh (Hills of the Ladder), the ladder being a pass from Glenlivet to Strathdon.

Laich of Moray

Laich in Scots means lowland and is possibly cognate with Gaelic leac [lek] (flat).

Lairig Ghru

This is old Gaelic làirig [lah-rig] (pass) and grù (surly), a fitting name as those who have passed through here in winter months will readily attest.

Logie

From Gaelic lagaigh [lakee] (place of the hollow).

Longmorn

From old Gaelic or Cumbric lann [lown] (church) and the personal name Morgan.

Maggieknockater

From Gaelic magh [mahG] (plain) and an fhùcadair [uhn ookatir] (of the fuller). So: fuller's plain. (A fuller is/was someone who cleans and thickens cloth.)

Nairn

This was first the name of the river, then applied to the town that stands at its mouth. The Gaelic name is Inbhir Nàrann. The name is of pre-Celtic origin. And its meaning? Did it ever have one?

Pittendreich

Nothing to do with the modern Scots word dreich (wet and dismal). This is from an older Gaelic sense of dreach [drehK] (beauty) preceded by na (of) and the common Pictish prefix pit, which means piece of land. Not a lot of existing names refer to the aesthetic as opposed to the topographical. This is a kind of Gaelico-Pictish Beaulieu, although to the modern (Scottish) ear it sounds like the opposite.

Pluscarden

From Brittonic-Pictish *plas* (place) and *cardden* (thicket).

> *Pluscarden Abbey is a 13th century monastery.*

Portessie

From Gaelic *port* (port) and *easach* [esoK] (with many waterfalls).

Rafford

No ford here, this is from Gaelic *ràth* [ra] (circular fort) and *àrd* [ahrt] (high). The f was already present around 1700 when the name was Raffart.

Rothes

From Gaelic *ràth* [ra] (ring fort).

> *There are four distilleries at Rothes: Glen Grant and Glenrothes, Glen Spey and Speyburn.*

Rothiemurcus

From Gaelic *ràth* [ra] (ring fort) and the old personal name *Muirgus*.

Spey, River

Of uncertain ancient origin, like most names of such great watercourses. This is the fastest flowing river in Scotland.

Spynie, Loch

This is thought to be connected with old Gaelic *spin* [speen] (thorn).

Tomintoul [pronounced tomin-towel]

From Gaelic *tom* (hillock) and *an t-sabhail* [uhn ta-uhl] (of the barn). So: Barnhill

Urquhart [pronounced URkurt]

Thought to be from Brittonic-Pictish *air* (on) and *cardden* (wood). So, roughly: Woodside.

Aberdeenshire
~ North

Bennachie

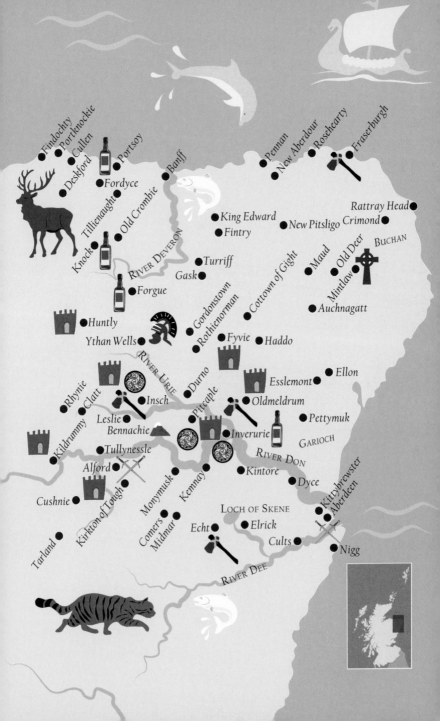

Aberdeen

Aber is Brittonic-Pictish for river mouth. You'd think the −deen element would refer to the river Dee that runs into the sea in Aberdeen. But no, the name was originally Aberdon (12th century) and refers to the settlement at the mouth of the Don, just to the north. And the locals are, of course, Aberdonians.

> *The Battle of Aberdeen was fought out between Royalist and Covenanter forces in the year 1644.*

Alford [pronounced aa-ford]

Some say this is from Gaelic *àth* [ah] (ford) with *àrd* [ahrt] (high). But it seems more likely that the English *ford* has just been tagged onto the Gaelic for ford by those incomers for whom the the word *àth* had no meaning. The place is on record as Afford in the early 13th century. The l just happened.

> *Craigievar Castle sits 5 miles to the south of Alford.*

> *The Battle of Alford was fought in 1645 between Royalists and Scots Covenanters.*

> *A life-sized statue of a bull speaks for this little town of Alford's claim to fame as the home of the Aberdeen Angus, first bred here by a local farmer, and now a worldwide favourite for steaks.*

Auchnagatt

From Gaelic *achadh* [ahK-uhG] (field), *na cat* (of the cat). Presumably a haunt of wildcats in days gone by.

Banff

The Gaelic *banbh* [ban-uhv] can mean both fallow land and pig.

Bennachie

From Gaelic *beinn* [bayn] (mountain) and *na cìche* [keeKuh] (of the breast).

Buchan

From Brittonic *buwch* (cow) and the suffix −*an* for a place.

Clatt
From Old Norse *klettr* (cliff, rocks).

Comers
From Gaelic *comar* [kohmuhr] (confluence of rivers).

Cottown of Gight [pronounced to rhyme with night]
The Gight is from Gaelic *gaoithe* [gur-yuh] (of wind).

Crimond
From old Gaelic *crech* [krehK] (summit) and more modern Gaelic *monadh* [monuhG] (hill, moor).

Crombie, Old Crombie
From Gaelic *crom* (crooked), doubtless referring to the winding stream. The –bie is less clear. It might be thought to come from the Old Norse *bú* (dwelling), as lots of such endings definitely do. But then a 1654 map shows this as Crommie, which suggests that the ending may simply be an ending meaning place. And if you say –mm– repeatedly it can turn into –mb–. But whether –bie or –ie, the place itself never grew; only its name spread far and wide.

Cullen
From Gaelic *cuileann* [kooluhn] (holly).

Cults
Probably from Gaelic *coilltean* [kuhl-tchen] meaning woods.

Cushnie
From old Gaelic *cuisneach* [koosh-noK] (frosty).

Dee, River
The belief is that this name is related to Gaelic *dia* (god). In ancient times rivers were seen as having divine status.

Deskford [pronounced deskart (by the locals)]

With neither desk nor ford in evidence, this is possibly from Gaelic *deas* [jes] (south) and old Gaelic *gart* (field), which does get close to the way the locals pronounce this name. Did some hard-of-hearing, deskbound clerk decide to anglicize it?

Deveron, River

Some think this is Gaelic *dubh* [doo] (dark, black) preceding *Èireann* (Irish), the river being so named by colonizing Gaels pushing eastwards. Others hold that the second part of this stems from *erin*, an ancient pre-Celtic river name, as found also in Earn (and in France in Rhône and in Germany in Rhine).

Don, River

It is thought that this name is related in its origins to the nearby River Dee, which has divine overtones (Gaelic *dia* being god). Almost certainly an older pre-Celtic name.

Durno

Gaelic *dòirneag* [dornak] is a pebble.

Dyce

From Gaelic *deis* [jaysh] (south).

Echt

German scholars might see a connection here with the German word *echt* (genuine). But Old English *eycht* means hilly.

> *Cullerlie stone circle, a couple of miles east of Echt, is thought to be some 4000 years old.*

Ellon

From Gaelic *àilean* [ahlen] (meadow).

Elrick

Likely from an old Gaelic word *eilreig* [elrek] (ambush), the ambush being a narrow or enclosed space which acted as a trap for finishing off hunted deer that were driven into it.

Esslemont

The Hill of Spells: from old Gaelic *eoisle* [yoshluh] (spells) and *monadh* [monuhG] (hill, moor).

Findochty [pronounced finnecty]

From Gaelic *fionn* [fewn] (fair) and *dabhach* [davoK] (an old unit of land measurement) and *taigh* [tY] (house).

Fintry

From Gaelic *fionn* [fewn] (white, fair) and Brittonic *tref* (homestead). The final f has been eroded over the past 800 years or so.

Fordyce

From Gaelic *deas* [jes] (south) preceded by old Gaelic *faithir* [fay-uhr] (slope). So: south-facing slope.

Forgue

Possibly from old Gaelic *fothair* [fohir] (terraced hillside) and Gaelic *gaoithe* [gur-yuh] (of wind).

Fraserburgh

No mysteries in this one, named thus in 1592 after Sir Alexander Fraser, the local landowner and town developer.

> *4 miles south of Fraserburgh is the Bronze-Age Memsie Cairn.*

Fyvie

Gaelic Fìobha [feevuh] is the name of one of the areas of ancient Pictland, which is thought to underlie the name of the district of Fife; and this village and castle, perhaps, only perhaps, share the same root.

Garioch [pronounced gairy]

From Gaelic *garbh* [garav] (rough) with the ending for a place *–ach*.

Gask

From older or more specialized Gaelic *gasg* (tail). A tapering tail of land coming out from a plateau.

Gordonstown

From Cumbric *gor* (great) and *din* (fort). Gordon is an element in a lot of placenames.

Haddo

In Gaelic a *dabhach* [davoK] is an old measure word used for land. A haddo is half of one of these, a half davoch.

Huntly

From Old English *hunta* (hunter) and *leah* (wood).

Insch

From Gaelic *innis* [eensh] which can mean both island and water-meadow.

> The Picardy Symbol Stone, just 2 miles northwest of Insch, is thought to have been set up by the Picts in the 7th century. Nearby Dunnideer is a prehistoric hill fort later converted to an early medieval castle.

Inverurie

From Gaelic *inbhir* [in-yuhr] (river mouth) and the name of the River Urie, which, at this point, flows into the Don.

> The Brandsbutt Pictish Stone is a mile to the north-west of Inverurie and the 4000 year old East Aquorthies Stone Circle a couple of miles to the west.

Kildrummy

From Gaelic *ceann* [k-yown] (head, end) and *druim* [droo-im] (ridge). The n has become an l.

Kemnay

From Gaelic *ceann* [k-yown] (head), and *a' mhaigh* [uh vY] (of the plain).

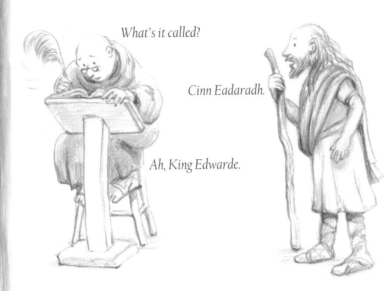

What's it called?

Cinn Eadaradh.

Ah, King Edwarde.

King Edward

Edward 1st or 2nd? Neither. This comes from Gaelic *cinn* (at the head of) and *eadaradh* [etruhG] (division, as in a division of land).

> *This tiny area around King Edward has given its name to a widely known variety of potato.*

Kintore

From Gaelic *cinn* (at the head of) and the old Gaelic *tòrr* (steep hill).

Kirkton of Tough [pronounced tooK]

The Tough is from Gaelic *tulach* [tooluhK] meaning hill or hillock.

Kittybrewster

From old Gaelic *cèide* [kayjuh] (green – as in a piece of land) and Scots *browster* (brewing).

Knock

From Gaelic *cnoc* meaning hill. The Gaelic is pronounced *crock*. It is strange that the name that has come down to the modern world is based on the English pronunciation and not on the Gaelic.

Leslie

Maybe from Gaelic *lios* [lis] (garden) and *linn* (pool). Or from Brittonic-Pictish *llys* (court) and *celyn* (holly).

Maud

Suggestions are Gaelic *madadh* [mat-uhG] (dog) or *mòd* [mawd] (court, meeting).

Midmar

Not the middle but from Brittonic-Pictish *mig* meaning bog. Mar is a 'county' of the ancient land of the vanished Picts. So: Bog of Mar.

Mintlaw

Law is a Scots word for hill and mint is mint, the herb.

> *Just west of Mintlaw is Deer Abbey. The oldest known pre-Norman text, the Book of Deer, was written by monks (10th century) on this site. The Book of Deer was written in Latin but it contains notes in the margins that monks added (12th century) in Gaelic. These are the oldest known Scottish Gaelic texts.*

Monymusk

From Gaelic *mòine* [mon-yuh] (peat) and an older sense of *mosach* [mosoK] (dirty).

New Aberdour

From Brittonic-Pictish *aber* (river mouth) and old Gaelic *dobhar* [doh-wuhr] (water). So: mouth of the water.

New Pitsligo

From the common Pictish prefix *pit* (piece of land) and Gaelic *sligeach* [shlig-uhK] (with a lot of shells).

Nigg

Possibly from old Gaelic *an ùig* [uhn oo-ig] (the cave, the hollow).

Old Deer

Nothing to do with animals. Deer is from Gaelic *doire* [doruh] meaning grove. There's also a New Deer. And the Forest of Deer is not what you might think.

Oldmeldrum

Gaelic *meall* [mel] (mountain) and *druim* [droo-im] (ridge) are possible roots.

Tolquhon Castle is 5 miles to the east of Oldmeldrum.

The Loanhead Stone Circle, 5 miles west of Oldmeldrum, is thought to be between 4000 and 4500 years old.

Pennan

This may be from Cumbric *pen* (head, top) and *an* (water, stream). The stream here flows into the sea from a steep headland. Most pen~ names are found much further south. In fact some would argue that this cannot possibly be a pen~ name for that very geographical reason, discounting the possibility of travellers taking names with them.

The village of Pennan leapt to fame as the location of the movie, Local Hero.

Pettymuk

From the old Pictish word *pett* or *pit* (place, piece of land) and Gaelic *muc* (pig).

Pitcaple

From the common Pictish prefix *pit* (piece of land) and Gaelic *capall* [kapuhl] (horse).

The Pictish cross-slab at Pitcaple, known as the Maiden Stone, dates from the 9th century.

Portknockie

From Gaelic *port* (port) and *cnoc* [krok] (hill) with the diminutive ending –ie tacked on. This might also be a Gaelic ending –aidh [ee], indicating place.

Portsoy

From Gaelic *port* (port) and *saoi* [sur-ee]. What's a saoi? Well the Nine Worthies in Gaelic are Naoinear Shaoidhean. And *saoi* is complex in meaning: good and generous man, valiant one, scholar.

Rattray Head

From Gaelic *ràth* [ra] (circular fort) and Brittonic *tref* (homestead).

Rhynie

From Gaelic *roinnean* [royn-yuhn] (a small portion of land).

Rosehearty

No roses, no hearties. This comes from old Gaelic *ros* (promontory) and the old Gaelic personal name *Abhartach* [avuhr-toK].

Rothienorman

From Gaelic *ràth* [ra] (circular fort), the fort once being held by Norsemen.

Skene, Loch of

Sgeachagan [skeKuhguhn] in Gaelic means haws, the berries of the hawthorn. The name Skene doesn't have a lot in common with the actual sound of the Gaelic but glosses over it in an anglicizing sort of way.

Tarland

From Gaelic *tarbh* [tarav] (bull) and *lann* (field).

Tillienaught, Tillynaught

Not nothing. From Gaelic *tulach* [tooluhK] (hill, hillock) and *nochd* [noKk] (bare).

Tullynessle

From Gaelic *tulach* [tooluhK] (hill, hillock) and older Gaelic *an eoisle* [uhn yoshluh] (of the spell). A kind of magic mountain.

Turriff

Locally pronounced Turra, this may well simply come from Gaelic *tòrr* (hill), with an ending indicating place.

Urie, River

One of several theories is that this name comes from Gaelic *iubhraich* [yew-reeK] (yew groves). But, as with many river names, this most probably pre-dates Gaelic and goes back to older Celtic or pre-Celtic times.

Ythan Wells [pronounced eye-than]

The Ythan is thought to come from an old Celtic word *iaith* meaning talk, with the addition of –an (often –on) indicating water. Burbling stream? But another theory has it coming from Brittonic *eith* (gorse).

Just to the east of this village of Ythan Wells are the remains of two Roman camps.

Mull &
surroundings

Calgary Bay, Mull

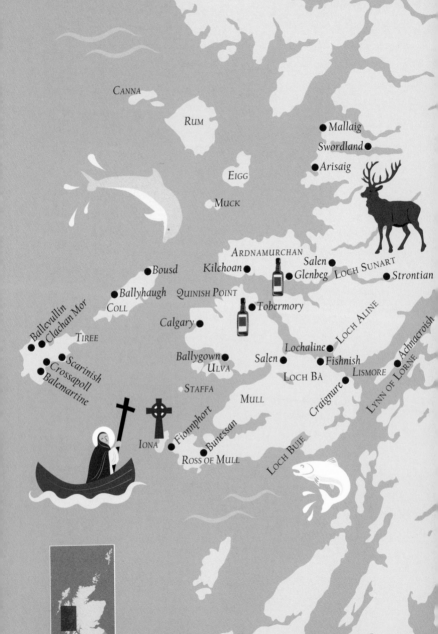

Achnacroish

From Gaelic *achadh* [ahK-uhG] (field) and *na croise* [nuh kroshuh] (of the cross). So: Crossfield.

Aline, Loch

From Gaelic *loch* and *àlainn* [ahlin] (beautiful).

Ardnamurchan

This is possibly from Gaelic *àird* [arsht] (height, promontory) and *nam muir-chon* [numoorKon] (of the sea dogs, the sea dogs being otters or possibly even pirates).

Arisaig

This is said to be from Old Norse *ár-óss* (river mouth) and a time-warped variant of *vík* to *uig* for the ending *–aig* meaning bay.

Bà, Loch

No reference to sheep here, but *bà* can mean 'of the cow' or, in old Gaelic, it can mean calm.

Balemartine

This is Martin's *baile* [baluh], his homestead or farm in Gaelic.

Ballevullin

This is the farmstead by the mill, in Gaelic the *baile a'mhuilinn* [baluh uh-vooleen].

Ballygown

There are lots of names starting with Bally– in Ireland but not just quite so many across the sea in Scotland. The Gaelic is *baile* [baluh], meaning home or farmstead and *a' ghobhainn* [Goh-een] means of the smith.

Ballyhaugh

The Gaelic *baile* [baluh] (settlement) by the mound. Although *haugh* is a Scots word meaning meadow this haugh is more likely to have come from the Vikings with their Old Norse *haugr* (mound).

Bousd

From Old Norse with contortions, *bólstaðr* being a farmstead.

Buie, Loch

Gaelic *buidhe* [boo-yuh] means yellow.

Bunessan

From Gaelic *bonn* [bown] (bottom) and *easain* [esin] (of the little waterfall).

Calgary

It's something of an exaggeration to call this tiny place a hamlet, a place whose name has spread to be attached to a sizeable Canadian metropolis. The −gary is very probably Gaelic *geàrraidh* [g-yahree], this in its own turn being loaned from Old Norse *gerði*, both meaning an enclosure, hence land closed off for cultivation and food; and belonging, in this instance, to a certain Kal or Kali.

Canna

It it thought that this may be from Old Norse *kanna* (bucket, can). Can you spot the bit that looks like an Old Norse bucket?

Clachan Mor

Gaelic for Big Stone (or Big Hamlet).

Coll

From Old Norse *kollr* (bare top, rounded top).

Craignure

From Gaelic *creag* [krek] (rock) and *an iubhair* [uhn yew-uhr] (of the yew tree).

Crossapoll

The farm or Old Norse *ból* at the *kross* or cross.

Eigg [pronounced egg]
Possibly from Gaelic *eag* [ek] (notch). You can't miss it.

Fionnphort [pronounced finnerfort]
This is Gaelic, straight Gaelic, *fionn* [fewn] (white, fair) and *port* (harbour), the h being a grammatical requirement.

Fishnish
From Old Norse *fiskr* (fish) and *nes* (point).

Glenbeg
From Gaelic *gleann beag* [gl-yown bek] (little glen).

Iona
Originally know as Ioua from the Old Irish *eo* (yew). Monkish scribes switched the u to an n, whether with intent or in error, it is, of course, not known. Around

> In 563 St Columba set up a monastery on Iona, a base for the missionaries who had started converting pagan Scots and Picts to the new Christian religion.

1100 the name is recorded as Hiona-Columcille (Columcille being a name for St Columba – dove of the church). The Norsemen changed this a little to Icolumkill, the I being Norse *ey* (island). In the early 1800s the name reverted to Iona. In Gaelic it is known simply as Ì [ee].

Kilchoan
From Gaelic *cill* (church) and the name of an 8th century holy man, *Comgan*.

Lismore
From Gaelic *lios* [lis] (garden) and *mòr* (big).

Lochaline
The village has the name of the loch. Gaelic *àlainn* [ahlin] means beautiful.

Lynn of Lorne

Lynn is an anglicization of Gaelic *linne* which here means firth. So this name is really the same as the Firth of Lorne further down toward Mull. Loarn or Lorne was the son of Fergus of Ulster and, it is said, one of the Irish colonizers along the Scottish coastline.

Mallaig

From Old Norse *múli* (headland) and a *vík* to *uig* for –aig meaning bay.

> It was here at Mallaig that Bonnie Prince Charlie landed when coming back to the mainland from Skye in July 1746, on the run from the Redcoats. Hidden beneath a rug in the bottom of a boat, he escaped capture yet again.

Muck

From Gaelic *muc* which means pig.

Mull

There are various names in various languages that appear to tie in with the present English name of this island. In AD 150 Ptolemy referred to it as Maleos; Old Norse *múli* is headland; Gaelic *maol* [murl] can be cape or headland. The modern Gaelic name is Muile (which has no meaning). The origins of the name Mull may lie further back in time, along with the origins of the later languages.

Quinish Point

From Old Norse *kví* (cattle pen) and *nes* (headland, point). This place was originally, and for several hundreds of years, called by a name that meant Cattle-pen Point. But eventually that name, Quinish, lost any meaning, at least in so far as monolingual English-speaking mapmakers were concerned; and so the English word Point was added on to a now meaningless name, the Point just repeating the Gaelicized Norse –nish.

Ross of Mull

From old Gaelic *ros* (promontory, moor). What does the landscape suggest?

Rum

Both Gaelic *rùm* and Old Norse *rúm* means space or room, of which there is still quite a lot on Rum, but are these not both too obvious and odd to be likely roots? Some say the name predates Celtic times. For consideration: Ramsey on the Isle of Man (known as Rhumsaa in the now nearly extinct Manx language) is said to derive from Old Norse *hrams-á* (wild garlic river) (and hramsa is Old English for wild garlic). Wild garlic is found on Rum.

Salen

From Gaelic *sàilean* [sahlen] (inlet).

Scarinish

From Old Norse *skári* (young seagull) and *nes* (headland).

> *The Old Norse has survived up here. You'll hear people in parts of the north of Scotland using the word scorrie for a seagull.*

Staffa

From Old Norse *stafr* (rod, pillar) and *ey* (island).

> *Staffa is where you'll find Fingal's Cave, the inspiration for Mendelssohn's Hebrides Overture*

Strontian

Two theories. Either from Gaelic *sròn* [stron] (point) and *teine* [chenuh] (fire). The fires would have been beacons. Or it comes from *sròn an t-sìthein* [stron uhn chee-en] which means point at the fairy hill. The second theory ties in with the local Gaelic name.

Sunart, Loch

From an Old Norse name *Sweyn* and *fjǫrðr* (fjord). Sweyn's fjord was recorded as Swynwort in 1372 and linguistic transformation has whittled this down to the present name.

Swordland

Nothing to do with battles or clan warfare. The Sword– is from Norse *svarð* and is cognate with English as in grassy sward.

Tiree

From Gaelic *tìr* [cheer] (land) and old Gaelic *eadha* [eGuh] (aspen).

Tobermory

From Gaelic *tobar* (well – in the ground, that is) and *Moire* [moruh] Mary's. So Mary's well (Mary being the Virgin Mary).

Ulva

From the Old Norse name *Ulfa* and *ey* (island).

Southwestern Highlands

Glencoe

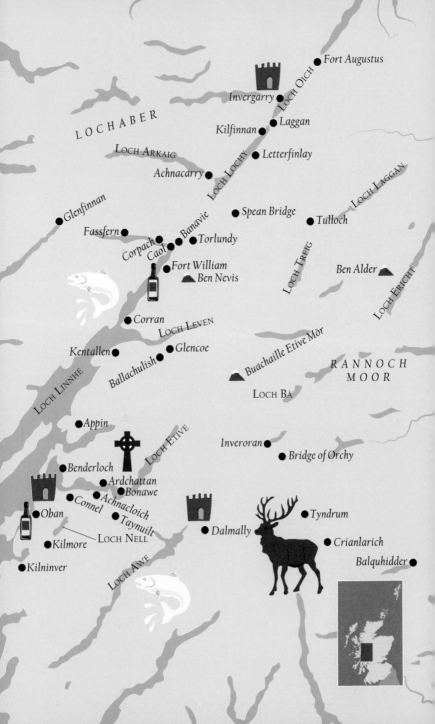

Achnacarry

From Gaelic *achadh* [ahK-uhG] (field), *na caraidh* [karee] (of the fish weir).

Achnacloich

From Gaelic *achadh* [ahK-uhG] (field) and *na cloich* (of the stone) [nuh kloyK]. So: Stonefield.

Appin

From an old Gaelic word *apainn* meaning abbey lands.

Ardchattan

From Gaelic *àird* [arsht] (promontory, height) and *Chatàin*, the name of a 6th century Irish monk who became a Celtic saint. So: Catan's height.

> *Ardchattan Priory Gardens were first tended by monks in the 13th century.*

Arkaig, Loch

Possibly, some say, from Gaelic *airc* (difficulty, distress), the difficulty being that of access.

> *It is said that Bonnie Prince Charlie's abandoned gold reserves are still lying hidden here in or around Loch Arkaig.*

Awe, Loch

Awesome yes, but the name is from old Gaelic *àbh* [ahv] which simply means water.

Bà, Loch

Well, *bà* means 'of the cow' or, in old Gaelic, it can mean calm.

Ballachulish [pronounced ballaHOOlish]

From Gaelic *baile* [baluh] (homestead, place) and *caolas* [kurluhs] (narrows).

Balquhidder [pronounced balwidder]

The common theory is that this is from Gaelic *baile* [baluh] (homestead, place) and *fodair* (of fodder). That certainly fits the nature of the terrain here. Old Scots *quhidder* or *fudder* (gust of wind) may well not be connected.

> *Balquhidder is the supposed burial place of Rob Roy (although more than one place make this claim).*

Banavie

The Gaelic *banbh* [ban-uhv] can mean both fallow land and pig. Pigs would seem the likelier naming source.

Head to Banavie to see Neptune's Staircase, a close-set series of 8 locks bringing the Caledonian Canal down to loch level in the West. It was built by Thomas Telford in the early 19th century.

Ben Alder

No connection with trees. The Alder is from old Gaelic *all* (rock) and *dobhar* [doh-wuhr] (water). One of the remotest Munros, Ben Alder's huge summit plateau holds a sizeable loch.

Ben Nevis

Possibly, it is said, from an old Gaelic word *nimheis* [neveesh] (venomous). But what is a poisonous mountain? There is an older pre-Celtic root form *nebh* (a Gael would pronounce this as nev) which is said to mean cloud, water, mist and which seems more plausible for the highest mountain in Britain. And the name of the mountain may well come from the name of the River Nevis, river names being the among the earliest names in the country.

Benderloch

From Gaelic *beinn* [bayn] (mountain) with *eadar* [etuh] (between) and *dà* (two) and *loch*. There is no s on loch because, in Gaelic, nouns after 'two' are in the singular and this Gaelic grammatical convention has been carried over into the anglicized form.

Bonawe

From Gaelic *bonn* [bown] (bottom) and *àth* [ah] (ford).

Bridge of Orchy

Orchy is the name of the river and, like many river names, of very ancient date and signification. The name is not unique. Down in Wales, in the Rhondda Valley, there is Treorchy, a settlement (Cumbric *tref*) by a stream called Orchy.

Buachaille Etive Mòr

The Gaelic means the big herdsman of Etive.

Caol

From Gaelic *caol* [kurl] (straits, narrows).

Connel

From the old Gaelic *coingheall* [kon-yahl], which means whirlpool.

Corpach

From Gaelic *corp* (corpse) and the ending *–ach* which means something like 'belonging to' or 'of'. Why? This was once a resting place for travelling funeral parties, before the dead reached their own last resting place.

Corran

In Gaelic a *corran* is a crescent or a sickle or a piece of land reaching out into the sea or loch.

Crianlarich

There are two contenders for Crianlarich. Either it's from Gaelic *crìon* (little) and old Gaelic *làirig* [lahrig] (pass). Or from Gaelic *critheann* [kree-uhn] (aspen tree) and *làraich* [lah-reeK] (of the site). You pays your money and takes your choice.

Dalmally

From Gaelic *dail* [dal] (field) and the old Gaelic personal name *Màillidh* [mahl-yee], an ancient holy man.

> *Kilchurn Castle is some two and a half miles west of Dalmally.*

Ericht, Loch

Two possibilities. Either it's from Gaelic *eireachdas* [ayruhK-kuhs] (attractiveness). Or it may come from an old Gaelic word *eireachd* [ayroKk] (assembly).

Etive, Loch

From an old Irish name *Eitig* (the foul one), a reference not to the loch itself but to a spirit said to live in its water.

Fassfern

From old Gaelic *fas* (place or, in names, stance) and Gaelic *feàrna* [f-yahrnuh] (alders). A stance was where cattle were kept overnight when being driven to market or other pastures.

Fort Augustus

Named after the Duke of Cumberland, famous for putting down the Jacobites, and whose first names were William Augustus. Its Gaelic name is Cill Chuimein (St Colman's church).

Fort William

Fort William is an erstwhile English garrison built in 1690 and named after the king, William II. The modern Gaelic name remains, bluntly, An-Gearasdan [an-geruhstan] (the garrison).

Fort William is home to the Ben Nevis distillery.

Glencoe

The –coe may be connected with an old Gaelic word *cumhang* [koo-ang] (narrow; gorge).

This is the scene of the Glencoe massacre in 1692 when Macdonalds were set on by Campbells.

Glenfinnan

Finan was a 7th century abbot from Ireland and a contemporary of St Columba.

The Glenfinnan Viaduct sprang to recent fame thanks to Harry Potter.

Invergarry

From Gaelic *inbhir* [in-yuhr] (mouth) and the name of the River Garry, which in turn comes from Gaelic *garbh* [garav] (rough).

Inveroran

From Gaelic *inbhir* [in-yuhr] (mouth) and old Gaelic *dobhran* [doh-ran] (water, stream).

Kentallen

From Gaelic *ceann* [k-yown] (head) and *an t-sailein* [uhn talen] (of the little inlet).

Kilfinnan

The *cill*, Gaelic for church or holy man's cell, of St Finnan.

Kilmore

A simple and straightforward description, this is from Gaelic *cill* (church) and *mòr* (big).

Kilninver

From Gaelic *cill* (church) and *an inbhir* [uhn in-yuhr] (of the river mouth).

Laggan (village and loch)

From Gaelic *lag* (hollow) and the diminutive ending *–an*. So: Little Hollow.

Letterfinlay

A letter to or from Finlay? Neither. From Gaelic *leitir* [letchir] (hillside) and *fionn* [fewn] (fair) and *laoich* [lur-eeK] (warrior's). So: Fair-warrior's-hill.

Leven, Loch

From Gaelic *leamhain* [levan] (elms).

Linnhe, Loch [pronounced linny]

Gaelic *linne* [leen-yuh] means simply pool or firth. The Gaelic pronunciation and the English are quite different; and the h in the English spelling of the name is puzzling. It's almost as though the h has been put there in a misguided attempt to make the word look more Gaelic.

Lochaber

Aber is an old Brittonic-Pictish word for river mouth or a place where two watercourses join. Here many lochs come end to end.

Lochy, Loch

From old Gaelic *lòch* (black, dark) and Irish Gaelic *dae* (goddess). Although Scots Gaelic is close with *dia* for goddess. This is a very ancient name going back to days of nature worship when streams and rivers flowed with the spirit of the black goddess.

Nell, Loch

This is swan loch, from Gaelic *nan eala* (of the swans).

Oban

From Old Norse *hóp* (shallow bay) or
Gaelic *òb* (bay) together with the Gaelic
diminutive ending *–an*. So: Little Bay.

> *Dunstaffnage Castle
> lies some 3 miles
> north of Oban.*

Oich, Loch

Possibly from the same stem as Loch Awe, old Gaelic *àbh* [ahv] which
simply means water, with the ending *–ach* for place.

Rannoch Moor

From Gaelic *raineach* [ran-yuh-uhK] (bracken).

Spean Bridge

The Gaelic diminutive ending *–an*, placed after Spe–, which probably
has the same origin as the River Spey.

Taynuilt [pronounced tie-nult]

From Gaelic *taigh* [tY] (house) with *an uillt* [uhn-oo-iltch] (of the
stream).

Torlundy

From Gaelic *tòrr* (hill, mound) and *lodan* (bog, small pool).

Treig, Loch

Modern Gaelic *trèig* means to abandon or desert. And deserted and
remote this loch certainly is, a focus of ancient Scottish folk tales of
kelpies or water-horses, taking people down to a watery death, and so
it is, some say, the loch of death.

Tulloch

From Gaelic *tulach* [tooluhK] meaning hill or hillock.

Tyndrum

From Gaelic *taigh* [tY] (house) and *na druim* [droo-im] which is an
older Gaelic form meaning 'on the ridge'.

Perthshire & surroundings

Blair Atholl

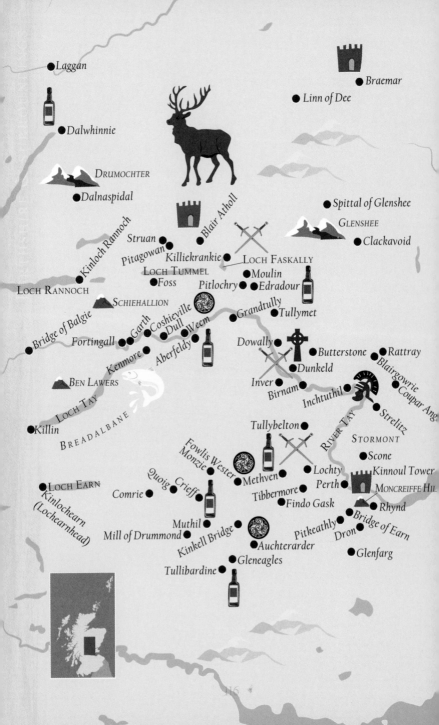

Aberfeldy

Aber– is from Brittonic-Pictish and means either river mouth or confluence of rivers. The –feldy comes from old Gaelic *Pheallaidh*, a form of the Gaelic name for St Paldoc, a Christian missionary who came to convert the Picts in the 5th century. But the name *Peallaidh* was also the name of a water sprite said to live here, where the Urlar Burn meets the Tay.

Auchterarder

From Gaelic *uachdar* [oo-uhK-kuhr] meaning upper land, *àrd* [ahrt] (high) and *dobhar* [doh-wuhr] which is old Gaelic for water. So: upland of high water.

In the village of Dunning, 5 miles east of Auchterarder, the Dupplin Pictish Cross is kept in St Serf's Church.

Ben Lawers

From Gaelic *labhar* [low-uhr], meaning loud (as the water in a stream).

Birnam

From Old English *beorn* (warrior) plus *ham* (village).

Birnam wood by Birnam was made famous by Shakespeare's Macbeth

Blair Atholl

Blair is Gaelic *blàr* (field, plain); Atholl is possibly from Gaelic *ath* (second) and old Gaelic *Fodhla* [foluh] (an old name for Ireland). Did invading Scots from the west leave a nostalgic name for this Pictish place?

Blairgowrie

Blair is Gaelic *blàr* (field, plain); the –gowrie part may be from Gabran, a king of Dal Riada in the west in the 6th century; the form *Gàbrain* [gahbran] is a genitive meaning 'of Gabran, belonging to Gabran'.

Braemar

From Gaelic *bràigh* [brY] (upland) and *Mhàrr*. Marr is the name of a district in Aberdeenshire.

Breadalbane

From old Gaelic *bràid* [braj] (mountainous country), which may well be an older form of *bràghad* [brah-uht] (upper part, top), and *albainn* [aluh-pin] (of Scotland).

Bridge of Balgie

From Gaelic *baile* [baluh] (homestead, place) and *gaoithe* [gur-yuh] (of wind).

Bridge of Earn

See Earn, Loch.

Butterstone

Bòthar [boh-huhr] in old Gaelic is either road or mud. And –tun is Old English for farmstead.

Clackavoid

It's all about turf and stone. *Clach* is Gaelic for stone and *na fòide* [na fawchuh] is Gaelic for 'of the turf'. Drop the n, sound the f like a v (which it almost is anyway), pronounce the whole thing as though it were English and there you are in Clackavoid.

Comrie

From Gaelic *comar* [kohmuhr] (confluence of rivers). The place suffers from flooding.

Coshieville

Looks like a French-influenced sort of name. But it's all from the Gaelic. *Cois a* [kosh uh] meaning 'beside the, near the' and old Gaelic *bhile* [veeluh] meaning thicket or clump of trees: so By-the-Thicket.

Coupar Angus

Actually now in Perthshire, although it was in Angus when it was thus named to distinguish it from the Cupar in Fife. The name is thought to come from an old Celtic word meaning confluence (of rivers).

Coupar Angus was the location of a major medieval monastery, very little of which now survives.

Crieff

From Gaelic *craobh* [krurv] (tree). A place amid trees. Or was there a special tree here?

Dalnaspidal

From Gaelic *dail* [dal] (field) and *nan spideal* [nuhn spijuhl] (of the refuge).

Dalwhinnie

From Gaelic *dail* [dal] (field) and older Gaelic *chuinnidh* [Koonyee] (of the champion). Ancient forms of Highland Games?

Dowally

From Gaelic *dubh* [doo] (black) and *aille* [Yl-yuh] (cliff).

Dron

From Gaelic *dronn* (ridge, hump).

Drumochter

From Gaelic *druim* [droo-im] (ridge) and *uachdar* [oo-uhK-kuhr] (upper land).

> *Drumochter is the main pass between the southern and northern parts of the central Highlands.*

Dull

Dull is from the Gaelic *dail* [dal] meaning field. You often get longer names starting with Dal– and these have the same origin.

> *Dull is tediously twinned with Boring in Oregon, USA.*

Dunkeld

From Gaelic *dùn* (fort) and *Chailleann* [Kalehn] (of the Caledonians). The Caledonians were Picts who had a fort here.

> *The battle of Dunkeld was a defeat for the Jacobites at the hands of the Scottish Cameronians in 1689.*

Earn, Loch

Thought to derive from a pre-Celtic root *ar*, which means flowing water (and may also lie behind the Rhine and the Rhône). But there is also likely to be a connection with Irish Gaelic *Eireann* (of Erin), Erin being a mythical goddess.

Edradour

From Gaelic *eadar* [etuh] (between), *dà* (two) and *dhobhar* [Goh-wuhr], which latter is an old Gaelic word for water.

Faskally, Loch

From old Gaelic *fas* (place) and *calaidh* [kally] (of the ferry). Loch Faskally is a 20th century manmade loch. The ferry, in its name, went over the River Tummel.

Findo Gask

Findo is from Saint Findoca. And the Gask is from old Gaelic *gasg* (tail), a tapering tail of land coming from a plateau.

Fortingall

From old Gaelic *fartair* [farsh-tahr] (fortress) and Gaelic *cill* (church, holy man's cell).

Foss

From Gaelic *fas* (stance, a place for parking cattle overnight).

Fowlis Wester

From old Gaelic *foghlais* [folish] (small stream).

> *A Pictish cross-slab can be seen here at Fowlis Wester.*

Garth

From old Gaelic *gart* (field, often used to mean a cornfield).

Gleneagles

Not a place where eagles once flew. From Gaelic *eaglais* [ek-lish] meaning church. So this is Churchglen.

Glenfarg

From Gaelic *fearg* [fer-uhg] which means anger.

Glenshee

From Gaelic *gleann* [gl-yown] (glen) and *sìth* [shee] which can mean either peace or fairy. Fairies are not that uncommon a feature in Gaelic placenames.

Grandtully [pronounced grantly]

Nothing grand. From Brittonic-Pictish *cardden* (thick; wooded) and Gaelic *tulach* [tooluhK] (hill, hillock). So: Trees-on-the-Hill.

Inchtuthil

From Gaelic *innis* [eensh] (riverside meadow) and *tuathal* [too-uh-huhl] (left-turning, anticlockwise). A further meaning of *tuathal* is unlucky or ill-omened.

> *Probably the Romans most northerly camp was built here at Inchtuthil in or around AD 83, to be abandoned a few years later. A huge hoard of buried nails was unearthed here in the course of excavations that started in the early 1950s. Over a million nails that the Romans obviously didn't want falling into the wrong hands (resource denial) and didn't want to lug away with them either.*

Inver

From Gaelic *inbhir* [in-yuhr]. Usually a prefix to longer names, *inver* refers to a place where two rivers come together or where a river flows into a loch or the sea. In English 'confluence' didn't really make the grade as a placename element, though of course 'mouth' certainly did.

Kenmore

From Gaelic *ceann* [k-yown] (head) and *mòr* (big). So: big head. The head will be a headland.

Killiekrankie

From Gaelic *coille* [kuhl-yuh] (wood) and *critheannaich* [kree-uh-neeK] (of aspens).

> *The battle here at Killiekrankie in the year 1689 was the first Jacobite uprising and a victory for the Highland Scots staying loyal to the Stuart King James VII against the Scottish Parliament that had given the crown to William of Orange.*

Killin

From Gaelic *cill* (church, holy man's cell) and *fionn* [fewn] (white). So: Whitechurch. But where has the f gone? Well, in Gaelic this is Cill Fhinn, and in that name the fh is silent. Killin is pronounced with the stress on the second syllable, matching its Gaelic origins.

> *The Falls of Dochart are a sight to see at Killin.*

Kinkell Bridge

From Gaelic *ceann* [k-yown] (head) and *na coille* [kuhl-yuh] (of the wood). So: Woodend.

Kinloch Rannoch

From Gaelic *ceann* [k-yown] (head), *loch* and *raineach* [ran-yuh-uhK] (bracken).

Kinlochearn

From Gaelic *cinn* (at the head of), preceding Loch Earn. The anglicized version of this name is Lochearnhead.

Kinnoul Tower

From Gaelic *cinn* (at the head of) and *aille* [Yl-yuh] (crag).

Laggan

From Gaelic *lag* (hollow) and the diminutive ending *–an*. So: Little Hollow.

Linn of Dee

Linne [leen-yuh] in old Gaelic means falls as in waterfalls.

Lochearnhead

This is an anglicized version of Kinlochearn, the village at the head of Loch Earn.

Lochty

From old Gaelic *lòch* (black) and Irish Gaelic *dae* (goddess). Although Scots Gaelic is close with *dia* for goddess. A very ancient name going back to days of nature worship when streams and rivers flowed with the spirit of the black goddess.

Methven

This is thought to originate from Brittonic *meddfaen* (middle stone).

> *In 1306 King Robert the Bruce suffered a defeat here at Methven at the hands of an English army.*

Mill of Drummond

From Gaelic *druim* [droo-im] (ridge) together with *monadh* [monuhG] (hill, moor). So: Ridge-backed hill or Mooridge.

Moncreiffe Hill

From Gaelic *monadh* [monuhG] (hill, moor) and *craoibh* [krureev] (of the tree). So: wooded hill.

Monzie [pronounced monee]

From Gaelic *magh* [mahG] (field) and old Gaelic *an eadha* [eGuh] (of corn). There is a record of this placename dated 1226 which has it as Mugheda, but that resemblance to a Gaelic origin has completely worn away over the centuries.

Moulin

No connection with French immigrant windmill builders. This comes from Gaelic *maoilinn* [murleen] which means a bare round hill.

Muthil [pronounced mew-thil]

From old Gaelic *maothail* [murhal] (soothing). A restful place to be in.

Perth

From Brittonic *perth* (thicket). We find *Pert* recorded as far back as 1128.

Pitagowan

From the common Pictish prefix *pit* (piece of land) and the Gaelic *ghobhainn* [Goh-een] (of the blacksmith). So: Smithfield.

Pitkeathly

From the common Pictish prefix *pit* (piece of land) and the Irish name *Cathalan*.

Pitlochry

From the common Pictish prefix *pit* (piece of land) and old Gaelic *cloichreach* [kloyK-ruhK] (stony place). The stones were quite probably stepping stones.

> *Dunfallandy Pictish cross-slab stands one mile to the south of Pitlochry.*

Quoig

Likely from an older sense of Gaelic *cuach* [koo-uhK] (hollow).

Rannoch, Loch

From Gaelic *raineach* [ran-yuh-uhK] (bracken).

Rattray

From Gaelic *ràth* [ra] (circular fort) and Brittonic *tref* (homestead).

Rhynd

From Gaelic *rinn* [rYn] which is a point (of land). The Gaelic name for this place is Rinn Dealgros, which is the point of the thorny wood.

Schiehallion

This might be from Gaelic *sine* [sheenuh] (breast) and *chailean* [Kalehn] (of a girl). Or maybe it is from Gaelic *sithich* [shee-eeK] (fairy) and *Chailleainn* [Kalehn] (of the Caledonians).

Scone [pronounced scoon]

From Gaelic *sgonn*, which means simply block or mound.

> *The Stone of Scone, on which ancient Scottish kings were crowned, was taken to Westminster Abbey in London in 1297, stolen/rescued by Scots nationalists in 1950 but is now back in Westminster again.*

Spittal of Glenshee

Not as nasty as it sounds. From the old Gaelic *spideal* [spijuhl] meaning refuge or spital. If you are going through Glen Shee without a car you'll be quite glad to come across Spittal of Glen Shee.

Stormont

From old Gaelic *stair* [star] (stepping stone) and *monadh* [monuhG] (hill, moor).

Strelitz

Sounds a bit Germanic? It is too. Named in honour of Charlotte, wife of King George III and daughter of the Duke of Mecklenburg-Strelitz, when a village for war veterans was built here in the second half of the 18th century.

Struan

From Gaelic *sruth* [stroo] (stream) and the ending –*an*, meaning little or –let.

Tay, Loch, River

The suggestion is that this is from a very ancient pre-Gaelic and pre-Celtic name for flowing water: *tau*.

Tibbermore

From Gaelic *tobar* (well – for water) and *mòr* (big). But some think it comes from *tobar* and *Mhoire* [voruh] and so means Mary's well.

Tullibardine

From Gaelic *tulach* [tooluhK] (hill, hillock) and old Gaelic *bàrdainn* [barteen] (of the warning). Quite probably a hill which was used as a place on which to light warning beacons. (These days *bàrdainn* is only in use on Islay.)

Tullybelton

From Gaelic *tulach* [tooluhK] (hill, hillock) and *Bealltainn* [b-yalteen]. Beltane was a Celtic festival when fires were lit to signal the start of summer.

Tullymet

From Gaelic *tulach* [tooluhK] (hill, hillock) and *mèath* (rich, as of soil).

Tummel, Loch

From old Gaelic *teimheil* [tevil] (dark or gloomy).

Weem

This is from Gaelic *uaimh* [oo-Yhv] (cave).

Aberdeenshire South
& Dundee
& Angus

Dunottar Castle

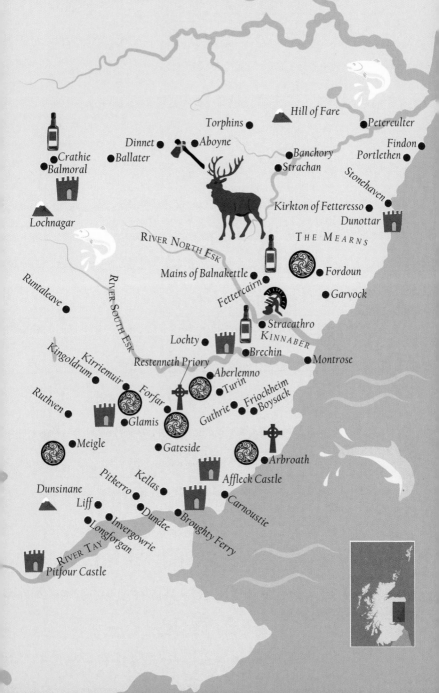

Aberlemno

From Brittonic-Pictish *aber* (river mouth) and Gaelic *leamhanach* [levuhnoK] (of elm trees).

Aboyne

Uncertainty surrounds this name. One theory is that is may be from Gaelic *àth* [ah] (ford) with *bò* (cow) and *fhionn* [yoon] (white). So: White Cow Ford.

Affleck Castle

From Gaelic *achadh* [ahK-uhG] (field) and *na leac* [lek] (of the flagstone), all a bit condensed with the passage of time.

Arbroath

From Brittonic *aber* (river mouth) and old Gaelic *brothach* [bro-uhK] which can mean either dirty or turbulent. You can see how both might apply to a river. Dr Johnson, on journeying north to Scotland in 1773, refers to Arbroath as Aberbrothick.

Ballater

From Gaelic *bealach* [b-yaluhK] (pass) and old Gaelic *dobhar* [doh-wuhr] (water).

Balmoral

This could be from Gaelic *baile* [baluh] (homestead, place) and *mòr* (big) and Brittonic *ial* (clearing). But it could also be from Gaelic *baile* (place) and Gaelic *mòrail* (majestic, magnificent). The present-day Gaelic name is Baile Mhorail [bal-uh vorel], which, strange to say, actually goes against the rules of modern standard Gaelic since the Mh– at the start of Mhorail should really be M–.

Banchory

From the Gaelic *beannchraigh* [byown-uh-Karee] (by the bends), the bends being in the River Dee.

Boysack

This is supposedly from the Gaelic *baile Iosaig* [baluh-eesak] (Isaac's town).

Brechin

Named, it is believed, after an ancient legendary Celtic hero, *Brychan*.

> *Edzell Castle is 6 miles to the north of Brechin.*

Broughty Ferry [pronounced brotty...]

The second part is simply the English word ferry. The first is from Gaelic *bruach-taibh* [broo-uhK-tayf] (bank of the Tay).

Carnoustie

There have been many theories, involving crows, pine trees, rocks and festivals. More likely ones: if it's from Gaelic *càrn* (hill) and *aosta* [ursta] (old), there's not much of an elevated landscape to back this up, apart from the higher ground at Laws. Another possibility is an old Brittonic-Pictish word *caer* (fort) together with a personal name. There's no fort there now, but a wooden stockade around a settlement would have qualified as a *caer*. The modern Gaelic name is Càrn Ùstaidh, but that appears to be just a transliteration of the English form. These are impenetrable convolutions of tangled reference. Anyone for golf?

Crathie

The general theory is that the name of this little place is derived from the Gaelic verb *crath* [kra] which means to shake. The reason for this connection with shaking is open to speculation. Some say it was down to boggy ground.

> The Royal Lochnagar Distillery is at Crathie.

Dinnet

From Gaelic *dìon* [jee-uhn] (protection, refuge) and *àite* [ah-chuh] (place).

Dundee

This is most likely to be from Gaelic *dùn* [doon] (fort) and a differently cast form of name of the Tay, which river's name itself is thought to derive from a very ancient pre-Gaelic and pre-Celtic name for flowing water: *tau*.

Dunottar

From Gaelic *dùn* [doon] (fort) and *faithir* [fay-uhr] (terraced slope above a beach). So the silent Gaelic –th– became a –t– and the initial f– dropped off.

> The castle here at Dunottar really has to be seen.

Dunsinane

From Gaelic *dùn* [doon] (hill, fort) and *sineachan* [sheenuh-Kuhn] (nipples). The old Gaels were mostly pretty dour and strictly topographical when it came to naming places. Not here in Dunsinane though.

> The place made famous by Shakespeare whose third apparition in Macbeth foretells:
> Macbeth shall never vanquished be until
> Great Birnam wood to high Dunsinane hill
> Shall come against him.

Esk, River

The South and North Esk have names from an ancient Celtic word *easg* (river). Gaelic *uisge* [oosh-guh] (water) is cognate.

Fettercairn

From old Gaelic *faithir* [fay-uhr] (slope) and Brittonic *cardden* (wood). So: Wooded Slope.

Fetteresso, Kirkton of

From old Gaelic *faithir* [fay-uhr] (slope) and *easach* [esoK] (waterlogged or, in current Gaelic, full of waterfalls).

Findon

From Gaelic *fionn* [fewn] (fair) and *dùn* (hill fort).

Fordoun

From Gaelic *dùn* (hill) preceded by old Gaelic *faithir* [fay-uhr] (slope).

> A Pictish stone, a cross-slab, can be seen in the parish church at Fordoun.

Forfar

From Gaelic *faire* [faruh] (lookout) preceded by old Gaelic *faithir* [fay-uhr] (slope). A good place to keep watch from.

> St Orland's stone, a Pictish cross-slab, stands 4 miles west of Forfar.

Friockheim [pronounced freekim]

An oddity, this. The –heim is German (home) and was put at the end of the name in 1830 by the landowner, one John Anderson, who had travelled in Germany and obviously liked the sound of the ending. The Friock– is either from the name of a Forfar bailie called Freke or is a corrupted form of Gaelic *fraoch* [frurK] (heather).

Garvock

From Gaelic *garbh* [garav] (rough) with the ending for a place –*ach*.

Gateside

From Scots *gait* (road) and *side* (area). So: roadside area (like calling a village Pull-in or Lay-by).

Glamis [pronounced glahms]

From an old Gaelic word *glamhus* [gla-uhs] (wide gap).

> The Eassie sculptured Pictish stone is in the old church just a mile west of Glamis.

Guthrie

From Gaelic *gaoth* [gur] (wind) and an older word *ruigh* [roo-ee] (slope). So: Windy Slope.

Hill of Fare

Fær is Old Norse for sheep – a possible origin.

Invergowrie

From Gaelic *inbhir* [in-yuhr] (mouth). The –gowrie may be from Gabran, a king of Dal Riada in the west in the 6th century; the form Gàbrain [gahbran] is a genitive meaning 'of Gabran, belonging to Gabran'. There is no river mouth here though.

Kellas

From Gaelic *ceall* [k-yal] (holy man's cell) and the ending –*ais* [esh], which indicates a place.

Kingoldrum

Royalty? No. This is from the Gaelic *cinn* (at the head of) with *coille* [kuhl-yuh] (wood) and *druim* [droo-im] (ridge). So: head of the wooded ridge.

Kinnaber

From Gaelic *ceann* [k-yown] (head) and Brittonic *aber* (river mouth).

Kirriemuir

From Gaelic *ceathramh* [keruhv] (an old unit of land measure equal to one quarter of a *dabhach* or davoch). The –muir is from Gaelic *Mhoire* (Mary's).

> *Sir James Barrie, author of Peter Pan, was born here in Kirriemuir in 1860.*

Liff

Quite likely from the Gaelic *luibh* [liv] (herb).

Lochnagar

This is not a loch but a mountain and the name is said to come from Gaelic *na gàire* [nuh gahruh] (of laughter).

Lochty

From old Gaelic *lòch* (black, dark) and Irish Gaelic *dae* (goddess). Although Scots Gaelic is close with *dia* for goddess. This is a very ancient name going back to days of nature worship when streams and rivers flowed with the spirit of the black goddess.

Longforgan

This is likely to be from old Gaelic *lann* [lown] (churchland), *for* (above) and old Gaelic *gronn* (marsh). (The lann is related to Welsh *llan*, which is land that has been cleared around a church.)

Mains of Balnakettle

The term Mains refers to the main farm of an estate. This was probably the main farm by the settlement or Gaelic *baile* [baluh] of a man called Catel.

Mearns, The [pronounced mairns]

From Gaelic *a' mhaoirne* [uh-vuhrnyuh] a district managed by a steward or *maor* [muhr] on behalf of the owner.

Meigle

Boggy field, from Brittonic-Pictish *mig* (swamp) and Brittonic-Pictish *dol* (field).

> *When in Meigle, head for the museum of sculptured Pictish stones.*

Montrose

From Gaelic *mòine* [mon-yuh] (peat) and old Gaelic *ros* (promontory).

Peterculter

The –culter is from Gaelic *cuil* [kool] (corner) and *tìr* [cheer] (land). Peter is St Peter.

Pitfour Castle

From the common Pictish prefix *pit* (piece of land) and a conjectured Gaelicized form *phùir* [foor] (of the crop land). Gaelic has *por* meaning crops or seed. It is thought that the word *pur* is related and possibly Pictish in origin.

Pitkerro

From the common Pictish prefix *pit* (piece of land) and Gaelic *ceathramh* [keruhv] (quarter, a unit of land equal to one quarter of an old unit of measurement, the davoch). Now part of Dundee.

Portlethen

From Gaelic *port* (port) and *leathan* [leh-huhn] (broad). A nice example of how Scots or English pronunciation was superimposed on the Gaelic (which doesn't have the th sound).

Restenneth Priory

From Brittonic-Pictish *ros* (moor) and *tened* (of fire).

Runtaleave

Maybe from Gaelic *raon* [rurn] (field) *dà shliabh* [da lee-uhv] (two hillsides).

Ruthven [pronounced rivven]

From Gaelic *ruadh* [roo-uhG] (red) and *abhainn* [avin] (river).

Stonehaven

With its old English *stan* or Scots *stane*, this is a harbour that offered a solid stony bed for ships and cargoes.

Stracathro

From Gaelic *srath* [stra] (wide river valley) (which in this name has lost its th sound, which is not present in the Gaelic. Candidates for the second element are Gaelic *cathrach* [karoK] which can mean 'of the seat' and old Gaelic *càtharach* [kahuhroK] (wet and mossy).

> *A Roman marching camp has been discovered at Stracathro.*

Strachan

From Gaelic *srath* [stra] (wide river valley) and what was possibly a diminutive ending –*an*.

Tay, Loch, River

The suggestion is that this is from a very ancient pre-Gaelic and pre-Celtic name for flowing water: *tau*.

Torphins

From Gaelic *tòrr* (hill) and *fionn* [fewn] (white, fair).

Turin

No, nothing Italian. This is from Gaelic *torran* (little hill).

Argyll ~ West

Cable Bay, Colonsay

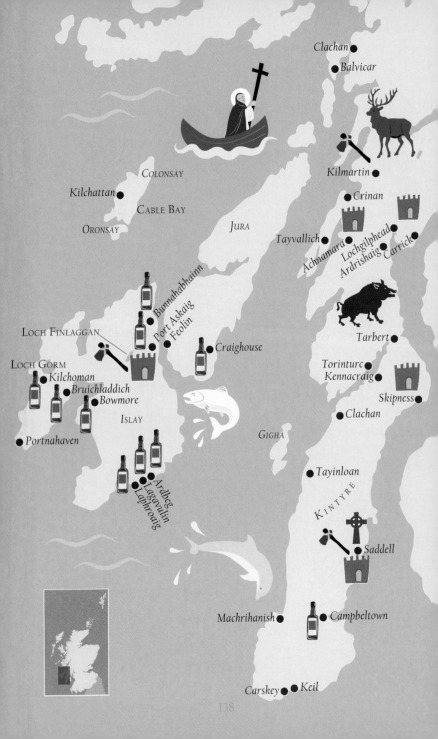

Achnamara

This is straight
Gaelic, the *achadh*
[ahK-uhG] *na mara*,
the field of the sea.

*Castle Sween is just south of Achnamara
on the banks of Loch Sween (that loch being
named after a Norseman Svein).*

Ardbeg

From Gaelic *àird* [arsht]
(promontory) and *beag* [bek]
(little).

*The Kildalton Cross, 5
miles northeast of Ardbeg,
attests to superb 8th century
masonry skills.*

Kildalton Cross, detail

Ardrishaig

Gaelic *àrd* [ahrt] (high), *dris* [drish] (brambles) and the ending *–aig* that derives from Old Norse *vík* (bay). So: High-brambles-on-sea.

Balvicar

From Gaelic, the vicar's farmstead, his *baile* [baluh].

Bowmore

From old Gaelic *both* [bo] (hut, house) and *mòr* (big). It may also be from Gaelic *bogha* [bo-uh](reef, submerged rock) and *mòr*.

Bruichladdich

Gaelic *Bruach a' Chladaich* [broo-uhK uh-KlateeK] (bank of the shore).

Bunnahabhainn [pronounced bunna-ha-vin]

From Gaelic *bonn* [bown] (bottom, end) and *na abhainn* [na avin] (of the river).

Cable Bay

The name of this local beauty spot stems from a reference to horses not cables. The wider bay on this coast is called in Gaelic Bàgh nan Capall [bahG nuhn kapuhl] which means Bay of the Horses. The English pronunciation has been superimposed on the Gaelic.

Campbeltown

No mysteries. Named after the Earl of Argyll, Archibald Campbell.

Carrick

From Gaelic *carraig* [karik] (rock, crag).

Carskey

A mutation from Gaelic *carraig sgèithe* [karak skay-uh] (wing rock).

Clachan

This is a fairly frequently found placename and two Clachans are shown on the map for this area. The name is from Gaelic *clachan* (stones). Were the houses here once notable for being built of stone? Or was it a good place to quarry stones? Or both? Clachan in Gaelic also means hamlet and, in older Gaelic, church graveyard.

Colonsay

The *ay* is from Old Norse *ey* (island) and the Colon(s) is thought perhaps to refer to St Columba, though there was equally possibly an Old Norseman who gave his name to the island.

Craighouse

A mixture of English *house* and Gaelic *creag* (rock, cliff). Or just crag.

Crinan

The Creones were an ancient tribe known only through a reference made by Ptolemy in around AD 150. Although Ptolemy had them quite a way further north, they may have been the source of this name.

Feolin

Old Gaelic *faolainn* [fuh-leen] is a stony beach. Just the right place for the ferry.

Finlaggan, Loch

From Gaelic *fionn* [fewn] (fair) and *lagan* (hollow, dell).

> The little island known as Council Isle in Loch Finlaggan was a place of great ceremonial importance in medieval Scotland, the place where the Lords of the Isles were installed. Evidence of Bronze-Age habitation here has also been unearthed.

Gigha

This is thought to come from Old Norse *guð* (god) and *ey* (island). The pronunciation has travelled a long way but an early record has Gudey back in 1263.

Gorm, Loch

Gorm [goruhm] is Gaelic for blue. But the Gaelic word is also used to describe the colour of grass and the greenery of forests and hills.

Islay [pronounced: eye-la]

Ile was possibly a person and Old Norse *ey* means island. The s came in later, but to no purpose, since it is not pronounced.

Jura

The Gaelic personal name *Doiread* [doruht] plus the Old Norse *ey* (island) are said to underlie the modern spelling. As is, possibly more plausibly, Old Norse *dyr ey* (deer island).

Keil [pronounced keel]

From Gaelic *cill*. Often translated as church, a cill was more a holy man's rudimentary cell.

Kennacraig

From Gaelic *ceann* [k-yown] (head or end) and *na creige* (of the rock or crag).

Kilchattan

From the Gaelic *cill* (church or holy man's cell) of *Chatàin*, a 6th century Irish monk, who was made a Celtic saint.

Kilchoman

From Gaelic *cill* (church, holy man's cell) and the name of the Celtic saint *Coman*.

A good example of a Celtic standing cross can be seen here at Kilchoman.

Kilmartin

From Gaelic *cill* (church) and Martin, a French saint from Tours.

The area around Kilmartin has a great wealth of prehistoric monuments, cairns, carvings and standing stones.

Kintyre

From Gaelic *ceann* [k-yown] (head) and *tire* [cheeruh] (of land).

Lagavulin

From Gaelic *lag* (hollow) and *a'mhuilinn* [uh-vooleen] (by the mill).

Laphroaig [pronounced la-froyg]

From Gaelic *lag* (hollow), *a' mhor aig* [uh vor ek] (by the big bay). The *aig* is a Gaelic rendering of Old Norse *vík* (bay) but not a real Gaelic word at all. A tortuous history of pronunciation.

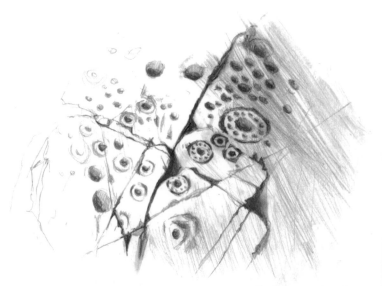

Cup and ring marks, Kilmartin

Lochgilphead

Gilb is Gaelic for chisel, which is how the shape of the smallish inlet off Loch Fyne was seen.

Machrihanish

Gaelic (and Scots) *machair* is the strip of grassy land just behind a beach. The second part of the name probably comes from an old personal name.

Oronsay

Odhran [oh-ran] was one of the twelve companions of the Irish Christian missionary St Columba. He died on Iona in the 6th century AD. So this island, as well as several others with similarly spelled names, is his island. The ending –ay is from Old Norse *ey* (island).

Port Askaig

One possibility is that this is from Old Norse *askr* (ash tree) and *vík* (bay), with the *vík* having undergone the typical mutation to –aig.

Portnahaven

From Gaelic *port* (port) and *na h-abhainn* [na ahvin] (of the river).

Saddell

This could be from Old Norse *sag* (saw) and *dalr* (valley), a place where timber was sawn.

> *The ruins of the Cistercian abbey here at Saddell date from the 12th century.*

Skipness

From Old Norse *skip* (ship) and *nes* (headland).

Tarbert

From Gaelic *tairbeart* [teruh-buhrsht] (isthmus, portage point). What's that? Portage points were important places in days when goods off a boat, or sometimes the whole boat itself, had to be dragged up the shore and overland to the next loch. Not surprisingly this is a common placename in Scotland.

Tayinloan

From Gaelic *taigh* [tY] (house) with *an lòin* [uhn lohn] (of the watery meadow).

Tayvallich

From Gaelic *taigh* [tY] (house) and *a' bhealaich* [uh v-yaleeK] (of the pass).

Torinturc

The Gaelic is *tòrr an tuirc* (boar hill).

Central Argyll

Machrie Moor, Arran

Ardbeg

A not uncommon placename, this is from Gaelic *àird* [arsht] (height, promontory) followed by *beag* [bek] (little).

Ardentinny

From Gaelic *àird* [arsht] (high point) and *an teine* [uhn chenuh] (of the fire). So a high point for a beacon.

Ardlamont

This the Gaelic *àird* [arsht] (height, promontory) of a Gael called MhicLaomainn [vik-luhmeen], known in English as Lamont.

Argyll

From a Gaelic word which, in its most recent form, is *oirthir* [or-heer] (coastland) and *Gàidheal* [geh-yuhl] (of the Gaels). It was the Scoti (that was the Romans' name for them) of Dalriada who were well established here before the end of the 5th century, and who called themselves Gàidheil (Gaels).

Arran

The name may be from Cumbric *aran* (height, peak). Or it may be from Irish Gaelic *arainn* (kidney), describing the line of the mountains. Both fit.

Auchenlochan

From Gaelic *achadh* [ahK-uhG] (field) and *an lochain* [uhn loKahn] (of the little loch).

Auchindrain

From Gaelic *achadh* [ahK-uhG] (field) and *an droighinn* [uhn droyeen] (of the thorn bush).

Brodick

From Old Norse *breiðr* (broad) and *vík* (bay). The v sound has been washed away.

Bute

Old Irish Gaelic *bót* (fire) has been put forward having Bute as a place where signal beacons were lit. The Norsemen called the island Rothesay, the *ey* (island) of a man called Roth, this name later being transferred to the main town on the island.

Cairndow [pronounced cairndoo]

From Gaelic *càrn* (hill) and *dubh* [doo] (black).

Cairndow is the site of the tallest tree in Britain (67 metres).

Colintraive

From Gaelic *caol* [kurl] (strait) and *an t-snàimh* [uhn tYv] (of the swim). The n in *snàimh* can be an r sound in some dialects. It was cattle that swam here, being driven across to the mainland from the island of Bute.

Corrie

Just what it says, the place of the corrie (a round hollow on a hillside).

Corriecravie

From Gaelic *coire* (corrie) and *chraobhaidh* [Kruh-vee] (tree place).

The Iron-Age Torr a' Chaisteal Fort stands just to the south of Corriecravie.

Dunoon

From Gaelic *dùn* [doon] (fort) and a form of an older Gaelic word *obhainn* [ohween] (on the river).

Eck, Loch

Possibly from Gaelic *each* [yaK] (horse). Whether an actual horse or the water-horse or kelpie of old Scots mythology is not clear.

Fada, Loch

Fada is Gaelic for long, the folk that named this loch had clearly not travelled very far afield.

Furnace

Yes, no catches! Named after the 18th century furnaces built here to smelt iron.

Fyne, Loch

Some would have this come from Gaelic *fion* [fee-uhn] (wine). But is that not a strange association? Also possibly from Gaelic *fin* [feen] which means white or fair.

Goat Fell

Either from Gaelic *gaoth* [gur] (wind) or from the Norse *geita* (goat). No goats these days but plenty of the former.

Goil, Loch

Goill in Gaelic means 'of the foreigner'. What intruders settled here? The foreigners here were likely to be Norsemen.

Holy Loch

Holy because of its links with St Mund, a follower of St Columba and bringer of Christianity.

Inchmarnock

From Gaelic *innis* [eensh] which can mean both island and water-meadow. The –marnock is from Gaelic *mo Iarnan* [mo ee-uhr-nuhn] (of my Iarnan – a priest) and the diminutive ending –oc. The priest's name also occurs in Kilmarnock.

Inveraray

From Gaelic *inbhir* [in-yuhr] (mouth) and *Aray* (a river name).

Kames

From Gaelic *camas* [kam-uhs] (bay, landing place).

Kilbrannan Sound

Kil– in placenames is very often to be derived from the Gaelic *cille* (church) but not so here where the Kil– comes from Gaelic *caol* [kurl] meaning straits or, as the English name has it, sound. The –brannan is from the name of an evangelizing Irish monk, Brénaind, who, in the 6th century, sailed with St Columba across these seas to Scotland.

Kilchattan

From the Gaelic *cill* (church or holy man's cell) of *Chatàin*, a 6th century Irish monk, who was made a Celtic saint.

Kilfinan

From Gaelic *cill* (church) and the name of St Finnan.

Lagg

From Gaelic *lag* (hollow).

> *At Lagg the Torrylin Cairn is a Neolithic chambered cairn. A walk inland leads to the Neolithic long cairn, Carn Ban.*

Lamlash

The name is thought to come from Gaelic *eilean* [aylan] (island), which has here lost its first syllable, and the name of a 7th century saint Molaise who lived in a cave on Holy Island.

Lochranza

The –ranza is thought to be from a form of Old Norse *reynir* (rowan tree) together with *á* (river).

Machrie

Gaelic (and Scots) *machair* is the strip of grassy land just behind a beach.

> *Auchagallon Bronze-Age stone circle stands just to the north of Machrie. And to the south is Machrie Moor: 5 Bronze-Age stone circles and the Bronze-Age cairn and stone circle of Moss Farm Road.*

Minard

This is from the Gaelic *mion* [min] (small, minor) together with *àird* [arsht] (headland, promontory).

Otter Ferry

Don't go otter-spotting. This comes from Gaelic *oitir* [otchir] which means sandbar or reef. And Ferry is just the English word.

Pirnmill

This stands out as being a relatively modern name. There was a mill here until 1849 that made pirns. Pirns? Conical wooden bobbins for the weaving industry.

Portavadie

From Gaelic *port* (port) and *a' mhadaidh* [uh vatee] (of the dog). (The dogs may have been wolves.)

Rothesay

This is from Old Norse *Roth* (a person's name) and *ey* (island) and was presumably at some earlier time used to refer to the whole Isle of Bute and not just to its main town.

Sannox

This has probably filtered down through the Gaelic Sannaig [shownak] which is itself a rendering of Old Norse *sandvík* meaning sandy bay. The English –ox ending would appear to be the result of an English s having been added to the Gaelic name.

Shiskine

From Gaelic *seasgan* [sheskan] (boggy place, reed grass).

> *The countryside around Shiskine is dotted with ancient stone circles.*

Strachur

From Gaelic *srath* [stra] (river valley) and *car* (twist). So: twisting valley. The nearby river Cur winds its way into Loch Eck.

Striven, Loch

The Gaelic name is Loch Sroigheann [stroy-uhn] but the meaning of that name is unclear and it may well be that it has no meaning. There are 15th century references to a vale of Stryne and a river Stryne and this name suggests Gaelic *sròn* [stron] (point), which in its genitive case is *sròine* [stron-yuh]. The present name may have emerged from this tangle via clerical error.

Strone

From Gaelic *sròn* [stron] which means both nose and point of land.

Stuck

Down the less travelled west shore of Loch Eck, this memorable name derives from Gaelic *stùc* (little hill). Anglicizing authorities shoved in the redundant k.

Thundergay

There are two views on this. Either from Gaelic *tòrr a' ghaoth* [tor uh gur] (windy hill). Or, more entertainingly, from Gaelic *tòn* (backside) and *ri gaoith* [ree gur-ee] (to the wind).

Tighnabruaich

From Gaelic *taigh* [tY] (house), and *na bruaich* [nuh broo-eech] (of the bank). Years ago there was just a single house here.

Toward

If you're heading toward Toward, be advised it rhymes with coward and is a name thought to refer to holes or caves.

Argyll ~ East & around Loch Lomond

Loch Lomond

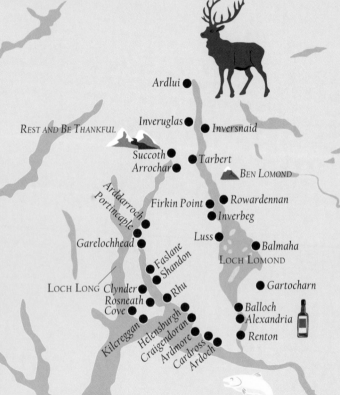

Ardlui

Inveruglas   Inversnaid

Rest and Be Thankful

Succoth   Tarbert

Arrochar

Ben Lomond

Arddarroch   Firkin Point   Rowardennan

Portincaple

Inverbeg

Garelochhead   Luss

Faslane   Balmaha

Shandon   Loch Lomond

Loch Long   Clynder   Rhu   Gartocharn

Rosneath

Cove   Balloch

Kilcreggan   Alexandria

Helensburgh

Craigendoran   Renton

Ardmore

Cardross

Ardoch

Alexandria

The town got its name from Alexander Smollett, local landowner and member of parliament, who developed the area with new housing for workers in the new factories in the second half of the 18th century.

Arddarroch

From Gaelic *àird* [arsht] (height, point) and *darach* (oak tree).

Ardlui

From Gaelic *àird* [arsht] (high point) and *laoigh* [lur-ee] (calf). A significant place for bygone cattle farmers.

Ardmore

From Gaelic *àird* [arsht] (height, point) and *mòr* (big).

Ardoch

From Gaelic *àrdach* [ahrtoK] (high place).

Arrochar

This is thought to be from a Gaelicized form of the Latin word *aratrum* (the area of land that 8 oxen can plough in a year, called a ploughgate in Scots).

Balloch

From Gaelic *bealach* [b-yaluhK] which means simply pass.

Balmaha

From Gaelic *baile* [baluh] (homestead, place) and the name of a Scottish saint, Mahew, sometimes referred to in Gaelic as Mo Thatha [muh ha].

Ben Lomond

see Lomond, Loch

Cardross

From Cumbric *cardden* (wooded) and *ros* (promontory).

> *Robert the Bruce died in Cardross in 1329.*

Clynder

From Gaelic *claon* [klurn] (sloped) and *dearg* [jeruhg] (red).

Cove

Easy. But no, it's not the English word meaning bay. Old Norse *kofi* means hut or hermit's cell. There are several Coves in Scotland.

Craigendoran

From Gaelic *creag* [krek] (rock) and *an dòbhrain* [uhn dohran] which can be two things: of the otter or, in old Gaelic, of the water.

Faslane

From old Gaelic *fas* (place or, in names, it can mean stance) and *lainne* [lan-yuh] (enclosed land). A stance was where cattle were kept overnight when being driven to market or other pastures.

Firkin Point

Hard to say anything about what the meaning of the Firkin Point is. But it's a good place for a picnic or a bit of a Firkin rest. Quite possibly they used to store barrels (or firkins) here, before loading or offloading.

Garelochhead

From Gaelic *geàrr* [g-yahr] (short). The –head is just a bit of English stuck on the end.

Gartocharn

From Gaelic *gàrradh* [garuhG] (garden, enclosure) and *càrn* (hump-backed hill).

Helensburgh

Named after Lady Helen Sutherland, whose husband, Lord Colquhoun of Luss, bought land here in 1752.

> *Helensburgh is the birthplace (1888) of John Logie Baird, one of the inventors of TV.*

Inverbeg

From Gaelic *inbhir* [in-yuhr] (river mouth) and *beag* [bek] (little).

Inversnaid

From Gaelic *inbhir* [in-yuhr] (mouth) with the name of the stream, the Snaid. Possibly from Gaelic *na snàthaid* [snah-uhj] (of a needle).

Inveruglas

From Gaelic *inbhir* [in-yuhr] (mouth), *dubh* [doo] (dark) and *glas* [glash] (grey, green), with the d gone begging.

Kilcreggan

From Gaelic *cill* (church) and *creag* [krek] (crag) with the diminutive Gaelic ending −*an*. So: Little Rock Church.

Lomond, Loch

Possibly from Cumbric *llumon* (beacon) with the loch taking its name from the mountain. The river flowing out of the loch is the Leven, and it does seem that in times past the loch itself was known as Loch Leven (Gaelic *leamhan* [levuhn] meaning elm).

Long, Loch

Long as it may be this comes from Gaelic *luing* [loo-ing] (of a ship).

Luss

From Gaelic *lus*, which means herb. This was a place where herbs were grown.

Portincaple

From Gaelic *port* (port), *na chapaill* [Kapuhl] (of the horse).

Renton

A member of the Smollett family, Mrs Jane Smollett, named this new town after her daughter-in-law in 1762.

Rest and Be Thankful

Named after the inscription left by one of those who built the first road over the hills from Arrochar toward Loch Fyne.

Rhu

From Gaelic *rubha* [roo-uh] (promontory).

Rosneath

From old Gaelic *ros* (promontory) and *neimhidh* [nevee] (of the church land). So: Holyhead.

Rowardennan

This is thought to be from Gaelic *rubha* [roo-uh] (promontory), *àird* [arsht] (height) and *Eonain* [yohnan] (of Eunan). But the ending may also be from a saint called Adamnan.

Shandon

From Gaelic *sean* [shen] (old) and *dùn* [doon] (fort).

Succoth

This may be from Gaelic *soc* which can mean snout, but the name here describes a pointed piece of ground where two streams merge – which sticks out like a snout. The –ach ending is added to denote place.

Tarbert

From Gaelic *tairbeart* [teruh-buhrsht] (isthmus, portage point). What's that? Portage points were important places in days when goods off a boat, or the whole boat itself, had to be dragged up the shore and overland to the next loch.

The Trossachs
& Forth Valley

Lake of Menteith

Aberfoyle

From Brittonic-Pictish *aber* (river confluence) and Gaelic *phuill* [foo-il] (of a pool) but *phuill* is more likely here to be in the sense of boggy field.

Alloa

From old Gaelic *alla-mhagh* [alla-vahG] (wild plain). Words can change shape with time.

Alva

From old Gaelic *ail-mhagh* [al-vahG] (rocky plain).

Ard, Loch

Àrd is Gaelic for high. *Àird* [arsht] meaning headland is less likely for this inland loch.

Arklet, Loch

The –let is probably from Gaelic *leathad* [leh-uht] (slope) and the Ark– from Gaelic *airc* (difficulty)

Balfron

This is the Gaelic *baile* [baluh] (homestead, place) of somebody whose name has been reduced over the centuries to *Fron*.

Bannockburn

From Cumbric *bannauc* (hill with a peak) and the Scots *burn* (stream) added. There are no peaks just here, though there are plenty visible in the distance.

> *In 1314 Robert the Bruce defeated the army of Edward II of England at the battle of Bannockburn.*

Ben Venue

The Gaelic name is A' Bheinn Mheanbh [uh vayn v-yehnuhv] (the tiny mountain). Take away the definite article and you have Beinn Mheanbh [bayn v-yehnuhv]. Apply a South Uist Gaelic accent and you get [bayn v-yehnoo]. Put the stress on the oo (where it doesn't really belong in either Gaelic or English) and anglicize it all a little and you get to Ben Venue.

Brig o' Turk

The Turks are not thought to have made expeditions this far north. The name's a mixture. Brig is Scots for bridge and Turk is from the Gaelic *tuirc* (of a boar).

Buchlyvie

From old Gaelic *both* [bo] (hut, house) and *slèibhe* [shlay-vuh] (of the slope).

Callander

From Brittonic *caled* (hard, rapid) and old Gaelic *dobhar* [doh-wuhr] (water).

Cambuskenneth

From Gaelic *camas* [kam-uhs] (bay) and an anglicized form of an old Pictish name, *Cinaed*.

> *Robert the Bruce's Parliament met in Cambuskenneth Abbey in 1314. And King James III and his wife Queen Margaret are buried here.*

Chon, Loch

Cu is Gaelic for dog or in older Gaelic for wolf as well. *Chon* is the genitive plural form making this the loch of the dogs or the loch of the wolves.

Clackmannan

From Gaelic *clach* (stone). The –mannan part is from the old Cumbric name for this part of Scotland at the head of the Firth of Forth and towards Stirling.

> *The stone of Mannan, named after the Celtic god Manau, can still be seen by the tolbooth in Clackmannan.*

Cowie

This may be from old Gaelic *coll* [kowl] (hazel tree) with an ending to indicate something like 'place of'.

Culross [pronounced kure-oss]

Fife's Hollywood, in name origin only. From Gaelic *cuileann* [kooluhn] (holly) and old Gaelic *ros* (wood).

Denny

From Old English *denu* (valley).

Dollar

Don't even think about it. A *dol* in Cumbric is a field and a *dol* which is *ar* is an arable field.

Castle Campbell sits up in the hills above Dollar.

Doune

From Gaelic *dùn* [doon] (hill fort).

Doune Castle sprang to fame as the setting for parts of the Monty Python film, Monty Python and the Holy Grail.

Drunkie, Loch

From a rarer Gaelic word *dronnag* [drownag] (little ridge).

Drymen [pronounced drimmuhn]

Scots without a drink? This comes from a form of Gaelic *druim* (ridge) with an ending possibly denoting place. So it means simply (and dully) on the ridge or ridge place.

Dumyat

From Gaelic *dùn* (hill fort) and the name of the ancient tribe of the Maeatae (a tribe recorded by the Romans). Dumyat with its twin summits marks the western end of the Ochils.

Dunblane

From Gaelic *dùn* (fort) and the name of St Blane who had his monastery here.

Falkirk

From Scots *fawe* (multi-coloured) and *kirk* (church). In the early 12th century the name was Egglesbreth which is, in modern Gaelic, *eaglais* [ek-lish] (church) and *breac* [brek] (multi-coloured, speckled). Sometime in the 12th or 13th century this Gaelic name was translated into Scots. The mix of different coloured stones used to build the local church clearly made an impact.

At the Battle of Falkirk in 1298 William Wallace's army was defeated by Edward I. Centuries later the Scottish Jacobites won a victory at the Battle of Falkirk Muir.

Fintry

From Gaelic *fionn* [fewn] (white, fair) and Cumbric *tref* (homestead). The final f has been eroded over the past 800 years or so.

Forth, River

River names are held to be the oldest names in the country, and some, like the Forth, cannot with any certainty be ascribed a meaning or a clear origin. It is said that the name might stem from an old Brittonic word (mooted as *voritia*) meaning slow-flowing; that certainly fits the nature of the river.

Gargunnock

From Gaelic *gàrradh* [gah-ruG] (garden) and *cnuic* [kroo-ik] (of the rounded hill).

Gartmore

From old Gaelic *gart* (field, cornfield) and Gaelic *mòr* (big).

Grangemouth

No mysteries here. The mouth of the Grange Burn.

Katrine, Loch [pronounced kat-rin]

This may be from Brittonic *cet* (wood) together with sources like those of Loch Earn: possibly a connection with Irish Gaelic *Eireann* (of Erin), Erin being a mythical goddess or a name for Ireland; or also possibly a connection with a pre-Celtic root *ar*, which means flowing water (and may have a connection with the Rhine and the Rhône).

This is the loch that supplies Glasgow's water.

Killearn

This should be from Gaelic *cill* (church) and *earrainn* [yar-uhn] (portion of land). But in the 13th century it was called Kynerine (head of the portion of land) with the *cinn* being Gaelic for 'at the head'.

Kincardine

From Gaelic *cinn* (at the head of) and Brittonic-Pictish *cardden* (wood).

Kippen

From Gaelic *ceap* [k-yep] (stump) with the diminutive ending –*an*. So: little stump, the stump being a part of the hills.

Lake of Menteith

A lake? But we're in Scotland! So why not loch? Well, this lake derives from an old Scots word *laich* which means low-lying ground.

> The remains of the 14th century Inchmahome Priory stand on an island in the Lake of Menteith.

Larbert

From Cumbric *lled* (half) and *pert* (wood). Gaelic *leth* [leh] also means half.

Longannet

From old Gaelic *lann* [lown] (enclosure) and *annaid* (church). The type of church is thought to be pre-Christian, the goddess being Anaitis, worshipped in the ancient Celtic world.

> Longannet was the home of a huge coal-fired power station – until 2016.

Lubnaig, Loch

From Gaelic *lùb* (bend). The ending is a diminutive form, the bent loch being only some 5km long.

Muckhart

Not a place where deer dung was stored. Muck– comes from the Gaelic *muc* meaning pig and –hart from old Gaelic *gart* meaning yard.

Plean

From Cumbric *plen* which means plain, flat land.

Polmont

From Gaelic *poll* (pool) and *monadh* [monuhG] (hill, moor). Or possibly also from *mònadh* (of peat).

Stenhousemuir

Whether you go with Old English or Scots it's all one: this is the stone house moor.

Stirling

This could be from Gaelic *sruth* [stroo] (stream, current) and *lann* [lown] (land). But the origins of this name are unclear. In the 12th century the town was referred to as Strivelyn, which some have interpreted as the dwelling of Melyn.

The Randolphfield standing stones are signs of the presence of Stone-Age man some 6000 years ago. They are now in front of the police station on the south side of Stirling.

The Battle of Stirling Bridge in 1297 was a victory for William Wallace over English forces.

Throsk

From Cumbric *tref* (house) and *usc* (river).

Tillicoultry [pronounced tilli-kootree]

From Gaelic *tulach* [tooluhK] (hill, hillock), *cùl* [kool] (back) and *tir* [cheer] (land). So: hill of the back land.

Tullibody

This is thought to be from Gaelic *tulach* [tooluhK] (hill, hillock) and *a' bhothain* [uh vohan] (of the hut). So: Huthill, although the pronunciation has changed more than somewhat.

Venachar, Loch

The horn-shaped loch. The Gaelic name is Bheannchair [v-yownuhKar] which means horned place.

Yetts of Muckhart

The *yetts* is a Scots word meaning gates or passes or way in. Muckhart comes from Gaelic *muc* (pig) and old Gaelic *gart* (yard). So: to the pig yard.

Fife ~ West

Scotstarvit Tower

Elcho Castle

Carpow

Abernethy

Auchtermuchty

Ladybank

Scotstarvit Tow

Strathmiglo

Kingskettle

Falkland

Freuchie

Kinross

Star

Loch Leven

Leslie

Markinch

Windygates

Kinglassie

Glenrothes

Crook of Devon

Cleish

Lochore

Loch Glow

Kelty

Cardenden

Loch Fitty

Lochgelly

Kirkcaldy

Dunfermline

Cowdenbeath

Auchtertool

Pittencrieff (Park)

Halbeath

Kinghorn

Aberdour

Pettycur

Rosyth

Burntisland

Dalgety Bay

Inverkeithing

Inchcolm

North Queensferry

Aberdour

From Brittonic-Pictish *aber* (river mouth) and old Gaelic *dobhar* [doh-wuhr] (water). So: Watermouth.

Abernethy

From Brittonic-Pictish *aber* (river mouth) probably joined with a Brittonic river name Nedd.

Abernethy was once a Pictish capital. In 1072 Abernethy was the place chosen for a meeting between King Malcolm III of Scotland and William the Conqueror, William being concerned about invasions of England from the north, something which Malcolm then undertook not to do, although his undertaking was of short duration. There is no connection (other than the name) with Abernethy biscuits.

Auchtermuchty

A pig-farming district, from Gaelic *uachdar* [oo-uhK-kuhr] meaning upper land and *mucadaidh* [mook-uhtee] (pig place).

The Romans built two camps in or around Auchtermuchty.

Auchtertool

Gaelic *uachdar* [oo-uhK-kuhr] meaning upper land and *tuathal* [too-uh-huhl] meaning anticlockwise or, in a figurative sense, awkward.

Burntisland

It is said that the name makes reference to the burning down of fishermen's huts on a little island which is now swallowed up in the harbour. The name didn't come into existence until 1586, the settlement and harbour having previously been known as Wester Kinghorn.

The Roman general Agricola had a camp built near Burntisland and made use of its harbour during his campaigns between AD 78 and 84.

Cardenden

Brittonic-Pictish *cardden* is a wood or thicket and the –den, which bears the stress in the pronunciation of this placename, is from Old English *denu* (valley).

Carpow
From Brittonic-Pictish *caer* (fort) and *pwll* (pool): fort on the pool.

> The remains of a Roman fort are to be seen here at Carpow.

Cleish
From Gaelic *clais* [clash] meaning trench, ditch or furrow.

Cowdenbeath
The –beath is from Gaelic *beithe* [beh-uh] meaning birch tree. The Cowden– is less clear. It might well be a person's name.

Crook of Devon
Devon is the river and crook is the bend in it, from Old Norse *krókr* (though English too).

Dalgety Bay
From Gaelic *dail* [dal] (field) and *gaoithe* [gur-yuh] (of the wind).

Dunfermline
From Gaelic *dùn* (fort) together with what is thought to be a Pictish proper name, possibly related to Farlane as in MacFarlane.

> Dunfermline Abbey is the burial place of Robert the Bruce and several other Scottish kings and queens. The town is also the birthplace of Andrew Carnegie.

Elcho Castle
This might be from old Gaelic *aileach* [eloK] (rocky), with the syllables twisted with time.

Falkland
Uncertainty reigns. It could be from Old English *falca* (falcon) or *folc* (people).

> Falkland Castle was taken over by the Scottish monarchy in the 14th century and refurbished as a Renaissance palace in the 16th.

Fitty, Loch
From older Gaelic *fòid* [foj] (peat) with the ending –*ait* [etch]: peaty place. This loch name has the same derivation as the Aberdonian Footdee, but down here in Fife the pronunciation has governed the spelling.

Freuchie

From Gaelic *fraochach* [frurKoK] (heathery).

Glenrothes

Not much ancient history in this one. The name was made up in 1948 when this new town was built. There is no glen here. There used to be a Rothes Colliery, named after a local landowning family.

Glow, Loch

The Welsh word *gloyw* (clear) points to a possible Brittonic or Cumbric origin.

Halbeath

From Gaelic *coille* [kuhl-yuh] (wood) and *beithe* [beh-uh] (birch tree). The modern pronunciation ignores the Gaelic origin.

Inchcolm

From Gaelic *innis* [eensh] (island) and the name *Colm*, which comes from St Columba.

> The abbey on Inchcolm was founded in 1123 and dedicated to St Columba.

Inverkeithing

From Gaelic *inbhir* [in-yuhr] (mouth) with the name of the river. The river name is likely to be related to the old Brittonic *coed* (wood).

Kelty

From Gaelic *coilltean* [kuhl-chen] (woods).

Kinghorn

Which king? None at all. From Gaelic *cinn* (at the head of) and what is thought to be a Pictish word taken over into old Gaelic, but not now in use, *gronn* (marshland).

Kinglassie

Named after a royal mistress? No, this is from Gaelic *ceann* [k-yown] (head) – here in the form *cinn* (at the head of) – and Brittonic *glas* (stream).

Kingskettle

Uncertainty reigns, but megalomaniac as some ancient kings may have been, naming a place after their kettle was probably beneath their dignity. There's an old Pictish name *Catel* and this may be a reference to his land. The Kings– may well be from Gaelic *ceann* [k-yown] (head), in its dative case *cinn* (at the head of).

Kinross

From Gaelic *ceann* [k-yown] (head) and old Gaelic *ros* (promontory). (Spithead might be a southern England equivalent.)

Kirkcaldy [pronounced kir-koddy]

No connection with the Kirk. From Brittonic *caer* (fort), *caled* (hard) and *din* (hill). So: fort on the hard hill.

> *Famous sons of Kirkcaldy include Adam Smith (the Wealth of Nations) born here 1723 and architect Robert Adam 1728; not to forget Gordon Brown, who, though not actually born here, did grow up here.*

Ladybank

There are two explanations of this, which may compete or may run alongside each other. One is that the name comes via a devious route from Gaelic *leathad* [leh-uht] (slope) and *bog* (boggy). But bog to bank is quite a leap. The other explanation comes in here. In the 13th century local monks were given the right to cut peat from a peat bog here and they named this place Our Lady's Bog, this name later being trimmed down to Ladybog. Subsequent sensitivities preferred Ladybank.

Leslie

Maybe from Gaelic *lios* [lis] (garden) and *linn* [leen] (pool). Or from Brittonic-Pictish *llys* (court) and *celyn* (holly).

Leven, Loch

From Gaelic *leamhain* [levan] (elms).

> *The castle here on Loch Leven can only be reached by boat.*

Lochgelly

White loch place. From Gaelic *geal* [g-yal] (white).

Lochore

Both the loch and the village names are probably derived from the River Ore, which, like most river names, is thought to date back to pre-Celtic times. It may have an origin in Brittonic *ara* (smooth flowing) (as does Ayr).

Markinch

From an older Gaelic word *marc* (horse) and (current) Gaelic *innis* (water meadow).

North Queensferry

Which queen? The place is named after Margaret, the second wife of King Malcolm III who reigned in the 11th century. The first ferry here was free and was provided for the benefit of pilgrims making their way up to St Andrews.

Pettycur

From the old Pictish word *pett* or *pit* (place, piece of land) and old Gaelic *ocar* [okuhr] (extortion). So a place with an extortionately high rent.

Pittencrieff (Park)

From the common Pictish prefix *pit* (piece of land) and Gaelic *na craoibhe* [krureevuh] (of the tree). This estate is now, very appropriately, a wooded public park.

Rosyth

From old Gaelic *ros* (promontory) and Old English *hide* (landing place).

Scotstarvit Tower

From Gaelic *tarbh* [tarav] (bull) and the ending *–ait* [etch] for a place. The first element, Scot, may be a personal name.

Star

Two related theories. From the Gaelic *staidhre* [sty-ruh] which means steps. And old Gaelic *stair* [star] means stepping stones or a crossing place over a stream or over a bog for cattle or sheep.

Strathmiglo

From the Gaelic *srath* [stra] (wide valley or strath) together with, it is said, Brittonic-Pictish *mig* (bog) and possibly a contracted form of *loch*.

There's a smallish Pictish stone to be seen near the cemetery at Strathmiglo.

Windygates

The gates here are not gates but a form of the Scots *yett*, which can mean either gate or pass. So: windy passes.

Fife ~ East

St Andrews

TENTS MUIR POINT

●Wormit

Leuchars ●

FOODIE HILL

St Andrews

Cupar ● ●Kemback

Ceres ●

●Pitmilly
●Kingsbarns

Dunino ●

Lochty ● ●Sorbie

●Crail

Kennoway ●

Largo

●Anstruther

Pittenweem

●Elie

Leven

Earlsferry

Methil

Buckhaven

Anstruther

This name comes from the Gaelic *an* (the) and *sruth* [stroo] (stream).
There may also be an Irish Gaelic influence here in *sruthair* [stroo-uhr]
(little stream).

Buckhaven

A buckie in Scots is a whelk. A lot of fishing went on here in centuries
past.

Ceres [pronounced like series]

This is not named after the Greek goddess of crops. Gaelic *siar*
(western) with the ending *–ais* [esh] (place) is the far more mundane
source.

Crail

From old Gaelic *carr* (boulder, rocky projection) and *ail* [al] (rock).
Records from 1153 have the name as Caraile, a name that time and
usage have caused to shrink.

> *The shipping hazard called North Carr Rocks lie off the coast here at*
> *Crail, the cause of many a shipwreck.*

Cupar

There was a theory, not held to be entirely satisfactory, that this name
was from a Gaelic word *comhpairt* [kohparsht] (common grazing
land). But it now seems far more likely to be the case that this is from
an old Cumbric word meaning confluence (of rivers), a very frequent
topographical feature behind placenames. And there are Welsh
cognates to be found in *cymer* (junction, of rivers) and also *cyffordd*
(junction, of roads).

Dunino

You don't know? It's from Gaelic *dùn* (hill) and *aonach* [ur-noK]
(moor).

Earlsferry

An English name going back to the 12th century when the Earls of Fife had set up a ferry service to take pilgrims, who were making their way to or from St Andrews, across the Firth of Forth to North Berwick.

Elie

One theory is that this is from an older Gaelic word *ealadh* [yaluhG] (tomb), although a connection with the name of the English cathedral city of Ely (place of eels) has also been put forward.

Foodie Hill

This is a common name element in these parts and it comes from the older Gaelic *fòid* [foj] (peat or turf) with the ending *–ait* [etch] indicating a place.

Kemback

From Gaelic *ceann* [k-yown] (head) and *bac* (hollow). So: head of the hollow.

Kennoway

This may well be from Gaelic *ceann* [k-yown] (head) and *achadh* [ahK-uhG] (field) although connections with a 6th century St. Kenneth have also been put forward. The ending *–way* seems to have just happened.

Kingsbarns

Well, this one is most probably just what it says: the site of the royal barns where grain was stored.

Largo

Nothing musical. The name of this popular little seaside town comes from an old Gaelic *leargach* [leruh-guhK] meaning steeply sloping.

> *Largo was the birthplace in 1676 of Alexander Selkirk, author of Robinson Crusoe.*

Leuchars [pronounced loo-kurs]

From Gaelic *luachair* [loo-uhKir] (rushes).

Leven

From Gaelic *leamhain* [levan] (elms).

Lochty

This is from old Gaelic *lòch* (black) and Irish Gaelic *dae* (goddess) or from Scots Gaelic *dia* (goddess). This ancient name harks back to days of nature worship when streams and rivers were seen as flowing with the force of divine spirits.

Methil

On the evidence of a 1250 written record which gives the name as Methkil this could be from Old Norse *mið* (middle) combined with Gaelic *cill* (church). This is just one of several theories.

Pitmilly

From the common Pictish prefix *pit* (piece of land) and Gaelic *muileann* [mooluhn] (of the mill).

The area around Pitmilly is a rich source of prehistoric artefacts from Neolithic times onward.

Pittenweem

Weem is from Gaelic *na h-uaimhe* [nuh hoo-Yvuh] (of the cave) preceded by Pictish *pit* (piece of land). So: place of the cave.

Sorbie

This is from the Old Norse (probably Danish) *saur* (bog) together with *bú* (settlement). The name is cognate with the English name Sowerby.

St Andrews

Named after its now ruined cathedral built in the 12th century and dedicated to Andrew, the patron saint of Scotland, whose bones were believed to have been brought here.

Tents Muir Point

Possibly from Brittonic-Pictish *dinas*, meaning fort and *muir* (Scots for moor).

Wormit

The origin of this name is uncertain. But it can be noted that wormit is Scots for wormwood, a plant used in making absinthe and in medieval times as a flavouring additive in mead.

> *Wormit was once a trailblazer as the first location in Scotland to have an electricity supply (from a windmill).*

Along the Clyde & into the Central Belt

The Necropolis, Glasgow

Airdrie

From Gaelic *àirde* [arshtuh] (height) and *ruighe* [roo-yuh] which is a
Gaelic word meaning forearm or, in placenames, slope. So: high slope.

Auldhouse

Too good to be true. No, *auld* is not old. Nor does *house* here mean
house. This name originally meant stream of the spectre and comes
from the Gaelic *allt fhuathais* [alt oo-ahish]. The anglicized or
Scotticized mask plausibly deceives.

Balmore

From Gaelic *baile* [baluh] (homestead, place) and *mòr* (big). It's a tiny
little place now.

Bearsden

There are several theories on this; here are two. First, not bears but
boars. The name comes from Old English *bár* (boar) and *denu* (valley).
Secondly, the name is old Scots, coming from *bear*, a variant of *bere*
(barley) and *den* (small glen). In any event, the name only gained
currency in the mid 19th century when it was transferred to the then
new railway station from the name of a nearby house (and small
district).

Biggar

Could this be Nordic influence a long way south? Is this Old Norse
bygg meaning barley together with *garðr* for field?

Blantyre

From Cumbric *blaen* (edge) and
Gaelic *tìr* [cheer] (land).

*The explorer and missionary
David Livingstone was born in
Blantyre in 1813.*

Bonkle

Could this be a sign of Roman presence? *Bona cella* would mean a good
place for grain storage. Another possibility is that this is from Gaelic
bonn [bown] (bottom) and *cill* (church, holy man's cell). As well as
Bonkle, there's a Buncle near Duns in East Lothian.

Bonnybridge

Just when you think you can work one out… No, not the place with a beautiful or bonnie bridge. Gaelic *buan* means long-lasting or durable.

Bothwell

From Old English *Buth* (a personal name) and *wael* (pool). But the Both– may also derive from Old English *bothe* (hut).

Bowling

Not an early centre for this sport. This is possibly from Gaelic *bò* meaning cow and *linn* meaning pond.

Busby

From Old Norse *buski* (bush) and *bú* (farm, place). So: bushy place.

Calder, River

From Brittonic *caled* (hard or stony, rapid) and old Gaelic (as well as Brittonic) *dobhar* [doh-wuhr] (water).

Cambuslang

From Gaelic *camas* [kam-uhs] (bay) and *long* (of ships). The Clyde was of greater importance here in olden days.

Campsies

From Gaelic *cam* (bent, curving) and *sìth* [shee] (hill). The Gaelic word *sìth* can also mean fairy and *sìthean* [shee-uhn] is a fairy hill.

Carluke

From Cumbric *caer* (fort) and *lwch* (marsh).

Carstairs

A daft name if you just stop to think about what its modern meaning would be. It's from Casteltarras, the name of a castle belonging to the bishops of Glasgow in the 14th century, which castle is now completely gone. In the 16th century the place was called Carstaris (getting closer).

Chatelherault

Purely French. One of the Dukes of Hamilton was made Duke of Chatelherault in the first part of the 16th century.

Cloch Point

From Gaelic *clach* [klaK] (stone).

Clyde, River

This is thought to originate from Cumbric *cloid* (the cleansing one). A different world that was.

Coatbridge

This is a mixture. Coat– is from Old English *cot* meaning cottage and the 16th century settlement was called just Cotts. The –bridge came later, when coal mining developed.

Condorrat

From Gaelic *comh* [koh] (coming together) with old Gaelic *dobhar* [doh-wuhr] (water) and the ending for place –*ait* [etch]. So: the place where two streams flow into one.

Croy

Thought to be from Gaelic *cruaidh* [kroo-Y] (hard). A reference to the ground perhaps?

Cumbernauld

From Gaelic *comar* [kohmuhr] (meeting, confluence) and *nan allt* (of the streams).

Dalmuir

From Gaelic *dail* [dal] (field) and *mòr* (big). It was recorded as Dalmore in the 13th century, before the Scots *muir* (moor) crept in.

Drumpellier

From Cumbric *din* (fort) and *peledyr* (of spears). Records have Dunpeleder in the 13th century but over the years the *dun* became *drum*.

Dullatur

From Gaelic *dubh* [doo] (dark) and an older Gaelic word *leitir* [letchir] (hillside).

> *A good stretch of Roman ditch is visible here at Dullatur.*

Dumbarton

From Gaelic *dùn* (fort) and *Breatainn* (of the Britons).

> *Dumbarton was the ancient capital of the Britons in the Kingdom of Strathclyde.*

Duntocher

From Gaelic *dùn* [doon] (fort) and an older Gaelic word *tochar* [toKuhr] (causeway, roadway).

Eaglesham

No, not a former home of eagles. This is a mixture of Gaelic *eaglais* [ek-lish] (church) and the Old English ending *–ham* for village.

> *Rudolf Hess parachuted down near Eaglesham in his misguided attempt to reconcile Britain to the Third Reich.*

East Kilbride

Kil– is from Gaelic *cill* which is usually described as a church, though in fact it was really a holy man's hermit cell. Bride is the name of a female saint *Brìd*, although originally *Brìd* was a pagan goddess.

Erskine

Maybe from Gaelic *àrd* [ahrt] (high) and *seasgan* [sheskan] (boggy place, reed grass). Or from Cumbric *ir* (green) and *ysgyn* (climb).

Giffnock

From Cumbric *cefn* (ridge) and the diminutive ending *–oc*. So: little ridge.

Glasgow

From Cumbric *glas* (green) and *cau* (hollow). (And modern Gaelic *glas* means grey-green.) The city has changed. But there's a good green hollow to be seen where the old town grew up between the cathedral and the Necropolis.

Glassford

This has nothing to do with either glass or fords. It's from Cumbric *glas* (green) and *ffridd* (wood).

Gourock

This could be from Gaelic *guireag* [goorek] which means pimple and could be seen as a joking reference, in evidence of ancient humour, to the wee hills above the town.

Greenock

Not green but sunny. From an old Gaelic word *grianachd* [gree-uhnaK] which means something like a warm sunny place.

Greenock was the birthplace in 1736 of James Watt, of steam engine fame.

Hamilton

The first Lord Hamilton, whose name is of Norman origin, moved up here from England in the 15th century and modestly renamed the existing village of Cadzow [pronounced cad-yow] after himself.

Houston

The *tun* (or, in Old English, farm) of Hugo.

Inchinnan

From Gaelic *innis* [eensh] (island) and *Finnén*, a personal name, usually now St Finnan.

Inchinnan is an older name for Glasgow International Airport.

Johnstone

From Old English, the *tun* or settlement of John.

Kelvin, River

From the Gaelic *caol-abhainn* [kurl avin] which means narrow river.

Kilmacolm

From Gaelic *cill* (church) and *Mo Coluim* [koluhm] (of my Columba – the famous Irish saint).

Kilsyth

From Gaelic *cill* (church) and a mystery ending. Kil– names often end in a saint's name, but St Syth is not known. Gaelic *saighde* [sYjuh] means 'of the arrow', but seems implausible. Perhaps an unsung holy man …

> *The Battle of Kilsyth between Royalists and Covenanters took place in 1645.*

Kirkintilloch

The Kirk– part is not the church. This name splits differently. It's from Cumbric *caer* (fort) together with Gaelic *cinn* (at the head) and Gaelic *tulaich* [tooleeK] (of the hill). If you go back to the 10th century this town was known as Caerpentaloch, all Cumbric. The shift from *pen* to *cinn* is common. The fort? That was put up in the 2nd century as part of the Roman defences along the Antonine wall.

Lanark

From Cumbric *llanerc* (glade).

Lenzie

Possibly originating with Gaelic *lèanaidh* [lee-ahnee] (watery meadow), this name has, over the years, been variously written as Lengze, Lenneth and Lingie. If the Gaelic origin holds good the z sound was never present in the name, but appears to have been introduced by clerical error or printer's error. And, unlike Culzean, the z here is pronounced.

Lesmahagow [pronounced lez-ma-hay-go]

Thought to be originally from Gaelic *eaglais* [ek-lish] (church) then undergoing a change to Gaelic *lios* [lis] (garden) plus a corrupted form of the name of St Machute.

Leven, River

From Gaelic *leamhain* [levan] (elms).

Milngavie [pronounced mul-guy]

Gaelic *maol na gaoithe* [murl nuh gur-yuh] (windy bare rounded hill) is one theory. *Muileann gaoithe* [moo-luhn gur-yuh] (windmill) another. And a third is *muileann Dhàibhidh* [moo-luhn GYvee] (Davie's mill).

Motherwell

More or less what it says. The town grew up around the site of a well dedicated to the Virgin Mary, Mother of God.

Paisley

Thought to be from Cumbric *pasgell* (pasture) and *llethr* (slope).

Paisley is the home of the famous Paisley pattern.

Renfrew

From Cumbric *rhyn* (point) and *frwd* (current). Logical enough: this town is located at the point where the White Cart and the Black Cart join the River Clyde.

Rutherglen

From Gaelic *ruadh* [roo-uhG] (red) and *gleann* [gl-yown] (glen).

Shotts

This is from Old English *sceots* (steep slopes).

Slamannan

The Sla– part is from Gaelic *sliabh* [shlee-uhv] (hill, slope); the –mannan part is from the old Cumbric name for the part of Scotland which was called Manau (around the head of the Firth of Forth towards Stirling).

Stepps

From the Scots word *stepp* which means a wooden stave. Laid crossways, these *stepps* make a road.

Strathaven [pronounced strayven]

From Gaelic *srath* [stra] (valley) and *abhainn* [avin] (river). The pronunciation of this town's name approximates the Gaelic, ignoring the pull of the English th.

Strathclyde

From Gaelic *srath* [stra], which is a flat river valley, and the name of the river, which is thought to come from Cumbric *cloid* (the cleansing one).

Tinto

Spanish red wine? No, this is from Gaelic *teine* [chenuh] (fire) and –*ach* [oK], an ending which makes the word an adjective. In the 19th century it was known as Tintock, which suggests a connection with the Gaelic *teinnteach* [chYn-choK] (fiery). The fire here would have been a signalling beacon. So: beacon hill.

Torrance

From Gaelic *torran* (little hill). An English plural –s has been added and then disguised giving a sort of French ring.

Twechar

This unusual name may possibly be a Scotticization of the Gaelic *tuineachadh* [toon-yuhKuhG] (though not based on the sound), which rather unimaginatively just means settlement.

> *This former mining village, Twechar, is a good place to head to if you want to see some of the remains of the Antonine Wall.*

Uddingston

In Old English the ending –*ing* means something like 'the people of'. So this is the *tun* (farm) of Oda's people.

Wishaw

From Old English *withig* (willow) and *sceaga* (wood). Shaw is Scots for wood.

The Lothians
~West

Cairnpapple Hill

Kinneil (House)
Bo'ness
Blackness
FIRTH OF FORTH
IRONGATH HILLS
Manuel
Linlithgow
Wester Ochiltree
Edinburgh
Arthur's Seat
Cairnpapple Hill
Broxburn
Ratho
Armadale
Bathgate
Livingston
East Calder
Mid Calder
Straiton
Whitburn
Roslin
Fauldhouse
Penicuik
RIVER ESK
Howgate
Leadburn
West Linton

Armadale

From Old Norse *armr* (arm) and *dalr* (dale, valley) but via Lord Armadale, who owned land here.

Arthur's Seat

Generally believed to be named after the King Arthur of legend.

Bathgate

So silly when you stop to think about it. But the words in this name have come a long way from their origins. Either Cumbric *baedd* (boar) and *coed* (wood) or Cumbric *bod* (house) and *coed* (wood).

Blackness

Old Norse *nes* and Old English *naes* both mean headland. Was the water here perhaps particularly murky?

> *Blackness was originally a port (in use from as far back as the 12th century) serving the royal palace at Linlithgow. The castle is sometimes referred to as the ship that never sailed.*

Bo'ness

Originally from Old English *Beornweard* (a man's name) plus *tun* (farm). This became modernized into Borrowstoun, a town which was a burgh, a town which had a charter. Being on a piece of land jutting out into the sea the ending *naes*, Old English for promontory (like the Old Norse for same) was added, but then the whole thing, seeing as it was a touch on the long side, received a trimming down to its present form.

Broxburn

This is said to be from Old English *broccs* (badger's) and *burna* (stream).

Cairnpapple Hill

From Gaelic *càrn* (hill) and Old English *popel* (pebble). But the –papple might also be connected with Old Norse *papa* (priest). So: Pebblehill or Priesthill.

> *Cairnpapple is an important prehistoric site, used for ceremonial and burial rituals from as far back as the 4th century BC.*

Calder (Mid and East)

From Brittonic *caled* (hard or stony, rapid) and old Gaelic *dobhar* [doh-wuhr] (water).

Edinburgh

From Cumbric *eiddyn* (rock face) and Old English *burh* (burg, town, stronghold).

Esk, River

From an ancient Celtic word *easg* (river). Gaelic *uisge* [oosh-guh] (water) is cognate.

Fauldhouse

From Old English *falh* (fallow land) plus house.

Forth, Firth of

It is said that the name of the Forth might stem from an old Brittonic word (mooted as voritia) meaning slow-flowing; that certainly fits the nature of the river, before it becomes the Firth.

Howgate

From Scots *gait* (road) in the *howe* (hollow).

Irongath Hills

Nothing to do with iron, this is from Gaelic *earrann* [yar-uhn] (area, portion of land) and *gaoithe* [gur-yuh] (of wind). The name is also written Airngath.

Kinneil (House)

From Gaelic *ceann* [k-yown] (head, end) and the old Gaelic *fàil* [fahl] (of the wall). Where has the f sound gone? Well, in Gaelic this would be *ceann fhàil* – and fh is silent.

Leadburn

Lead mining district? No, this is from Gaelic *leac* [lek] (flat stone) and the name *Bernard*. Records from around 1200 show Lecbernard. A *leac* can also be a gravestone.

Linlithgow

From Cumbric *llyn* (lake) with *lleith* (damp) and *cau* (hollow). So: lake in the damp hollow.

Mary Queen of Scots was born in Linlithgow Palace in 1542.

Livingston

Remarkably stable as a name. Down the centuries the e of the original Leving became an i. Records from 1124 show this as Villa Leving. And in 1688 the town is recorded as Levingston, the farm or settlement belonging to a certain Leving.

Manuel

No particular Spaniard. This comes from Cumbric *maen* (rock) and *gwel* (view).

Penicuik

From Cumbric *pen* (head, top), *y* (the) and *cog* (cuckoo). So: cuckoo hill.

Ratho

Gaelic *ràth* [ra] is a circular fort, and *ràthach* [ra-oK] describes a place which has a circular fort.

Roslin

From Cumbric *ros* (moor) and *celyn* (holly).

Home to Rosslyn Chapel, famous for its superbly executed stone carvings.

The Battle of Roslin in 1303 was a victory for the Scots over English forces.

Straiton

From Old English *straet* (road) and *tun* (farm or settlement). The *straet* here probably referred to a Roman road.

In the 2nd century AD there was a lot of Roman military activity in the area around Straiton.

West Linton

It doesn't sound very Scottish but then this is the part of the country where the Angles arrived, bringing their own idiom with them. The first half of Linton is from Old English *lin* (flax) and the second half from Old English *tun* (farm, settlement). (But there isn't always such a clear divide between languages: Gaelic *lion* means flax too.)

Wester Ochiltree

From Cumbric *ocel* (high) and *tref* (house).

Whitburn

From Old English *hwit* (white) and *burna* (stream).

The Lothians
~ East

Bass Rock

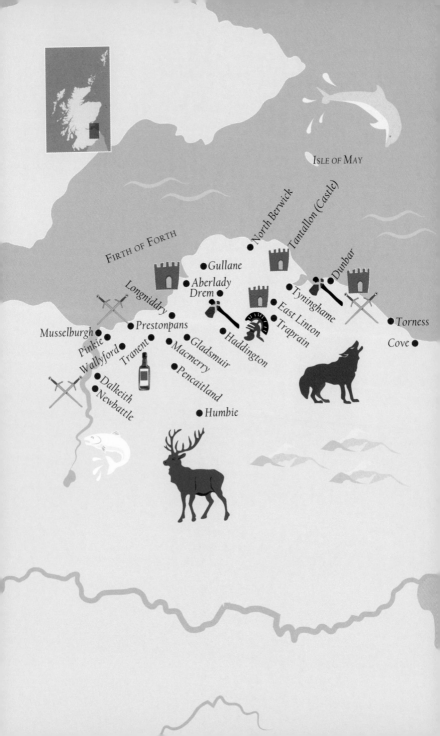

ISLE OF MAY

FIRTH OF FORTH

North Berwick

Tantallon (Castle)

Dunbar

Gullane

Aberlady

Drem

Longniddry

Tyninghame

East Linton

Traprain

Torness

Musselburgh

Prestonpans

Haddington

Cove

Pinkie

Wallyford

Tranent

Gladsmuir

Macmerry

Dalkeith

Pencaitland

Newbattle

Humbie

Aberlady

The Aber– is clear enough: it's the Brittonic-Pictish *aber* (river mouth). But the –lady is less clear. It might, it is thought, be from Old English *hlaedig* (lady) and indeed there are the ruins here of an old Christian chapel, with its naming asssociations of Our Lady. And in the 7th century Aberlady was a place of religious importance, having links with monastic centres in both Iona in the north and Lindisfarne to the south. Another theory has it that the Peffer Burn here was once known as the Leddie and that the –lady comes from this, a theory reinforced by the local pronunciation.

> *Gosford House lies a couple of miles southwest of Aberlady, towards Longniddry.*

Cove

Easy. But it's not the English word meaning bay. Old Norse *kofi* means hut or hermit's cell. There are several Coves in Scotland.

Dalkeith

From Gaelic *dail* [dal] (field) or from Cumbric *dol*, which means the same, and Cumbric *coed* (wood).

Drem

Another variant of Gaelic *druim* [droo-im] (ridge), remoulded by time and local speech.

> *Just south of Drem is the Iron-Age settlement, Chesters Hill Fort.*

Dunbar

From Gaelic *dùn* (fort) and Cumbric *barr* (height).

> *The once mighty castle of Dunbar was finally rendered useless in the late 16th century.*

> *In 1650, at the Battle of Dunbar, Cromwell's English army won a victory over Scots loyal to King Charles II.*

East Linton

The name sounds rather English. And so it is, coming from Old English *lin* (flax) and *tun* (farmstead). (Although Gaelic *lìon* means flax too.)

Hailes Castle stands just southwest of East Linton.

Forth, Firth of

It is said that the name of the Forth might stem from an old Brittonic word (mooted as *voritia*) meaning slow-flowing; that certainly fits the nature of the river, before it becomes the Firth.

Gladsmuir

From Old English *gled* (kestrel) amd *muir* meaning moor.

Gullane [pronounced gullan]

From Gaelic *gualainn* [goo-uhleen] (shoulder). The shoulder, that is, of a hill.

Haddington

In Old English the ending –*ing* means 'the people of'. So this is the *tun* (farm) of Hada's people.

John Knox, fierce leader of the Scottish Protestant Reformation, was born in Haddington in the early years of the 16th century.

Humbie

Thought to be from Old English *hund* (dog) and Old Norse *bú* (dwelling, village).

Longniddry

This is thought to be from Cumbric *lann* (church or churchland), *nuadh* [noo-uhG] (new) and *tref* (village).

Lothian

This name has no hidden meaning. It is thought to derive from a Brittonic personal name, *Leudonus*, said to be a long-ago king of Leudonia, a district in these parts. And the name Louthion, referring to these same parts, is recorded many centuries later.

Macmerry

Happily located not far from Gladsmuir, this is not a Scots surname but comes from Gaelic *magh* (plain). Old Gaelic *meurag* for small pebble is a possible explanation of the merry.

May, Isle of

Not the month. From Old Norse *már* (seagull) and *ey* (island). Spoken together this gives May – the Isle is of course a redundant addition.

Musselburgh

All Old English, the burgh or town for mussels.

Newbattle

Not military. Battle is from the Old English word *botl* which means house.

North Berwick [pronounced ...berrick]

From Old English *bere* (barley) and *wic* (farm).

Pencaitland

From Cumbric *pen* (head), *coet* (wood) and *lann* (enclosure). So: head of the wooded enclosure.

Pinkie

In Scots (and in some parts of northern England and the USA too) your pinkie is your little finger. Well, this has no connection with that. The name comes from Cumbric *pen* (hill) and a person's name *Cé*.

> The battle of Pinkie was fought in the year 1547 and ranks as one of the biggest battles, in terms of troop numbers, fought in Scotland. Some 20,000 Scots were defeated by some 18,000 English.

Prestonpans

From Old English *preost* (priest), *tun* (village) and the Scots *pans* (salt pans). So: priest's village by the salt pans.

> In the short battle here at Prestonpans in 1745 the Jacobites routed English government forces.

Tantallon (Castle)

From Cumbric *din* (fort) and *talgan* (high-fronted).

Torness

From Gaelic *tòrr* (hill, mound) and Old Norse *nes* (headland).

> *Torness is known for its nuclear power station, a clear landmark on the coastline.*

Tranent

From Cumbric *tref* (settlement, home) and *yr neint* (by the valley).

Traprain

From Cumbric *tref* (settlement, home) and *pren* (tree).

> *In 1919 a hoard of Roman silver was found on Traprain Law.*

Tyninghame

A very English name from Old English *tyn* (the river name) and *inga-ham* (home of the people). So: home of the people by the Tyne.

Wallyford

The Scots word *wally* means good or fine. So here was a good place to cross the river.

Ayrshire

River Afton

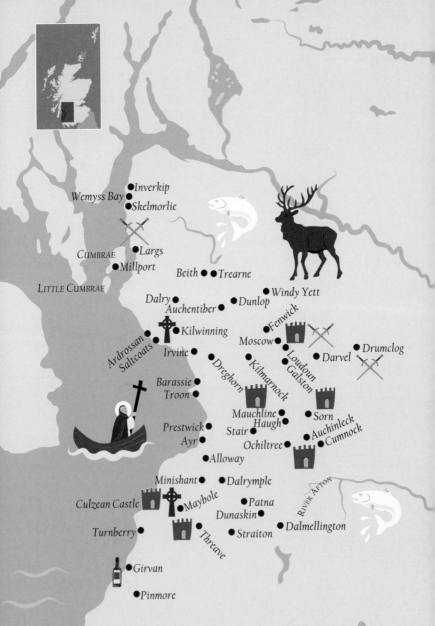

Afton, River

From old Gaelic *àbh* [ahv] (stream) and *donn* [down] (brown).

Burns made the river famous with his poem 'Flow gently, sweet Afton'.

Alloway

From old Gaelic *alla-mhagh* [alla-vahG] (wild plain). Words can change shape with time.

Alloway was the birthplace, in 1759, of Robert Burns.

Ardrossan

Possibly from Gaelic *àirde* [arshtuh] (promontory) and old Gaelic *rois* [rosh] (of the cape) with the diminutive ending *–an* (little).

Auchentiber

From the Gaelic *achadh* [ahK-uhG] (field) and a variant form of the Gaelic *tobar* (well, as in a hole in the ground).

Auchinleck

From Gaelic *achadh* [ahK-uhG] (field) and *nun leac* [nuhn lek] (of the flagstones).

Auchinleck is the burial place of James Boswell, the 9th Laird of Auchinleck and famously Dr Johnson's biographer.

Ayr

Named after the River Ayr. And this river name is thought to be from an ancient Brittonic word *ara* (smooth running).

Barassie

This is likely to be from Gaelic *bàrr* (top) and old Gaelic *fasadh* [fasuhG] (stance, a stance being a resting place for cattle drovers). The Gaelic would inflect as *fhasaidh* which, the fh being silent, would be pronounced as *–assie*.

Beith [pronounced beeth]

From Gaelic *beithe* [beh-uh] meaning birch tree.

Culzean Castle

[pronounced cull-ANE]
From Gaelic *cùil* [kool] (nook)
and *còin* [yon] (birds). Where did
the z come from? The silent z. The
underlying Gaelic name, Cuilean, is
pronounced with an l sound like the
ll in million: cul-yane. In medieval
times this 'yuh' sound was written
with a character called a yogh, which looked like a z with a long tail.
Printers who did not have both characters (the yogh and a z) just
used the z. And it has stayed there.

Cumbrae

The bigger island of the Cumbrians; from Cumbric *cymry* (Cumbrians)
and Old Norse *ey* (island).

Cumnock

From Gaelic *cam* (crooked) and *cnoc* [krok] (hill). Scots or English
pronunciation patterns have overruled the Gaelic.

Dalmellington

The Gaelic word *dail* [dal] (field, meadow) put in front of the town or
farmstead of Mel's people.

Dalry [pronounced dal-RYE]

From Gaelic *dail* [dal] (field) and *fhraoich* [rur-eeK] (heather). Or the
–ry element (which takes the stress) may be from Gaelic *ruighe* [ree-
yuh] (lower slope).

Dalrymple

From Gaelic *dail* [dal] (field), *crom* (bent, crooked) and *poll* (pool). So:
crooked pool field. The c of crom went missing.

Darvel

From old Gaelic *dobhar* [doh-wuhr] (water) and Gaelic *bhaile* [valuh]
(of the town).

Dreghorn

From Old English *dryge* (dry) and *erne* (house). But *dryge* can also mean fort.

Drumclog

From Gaelic *druim* [droo-im] (ridge) and *clog*, from a Brittonic word *colg* meaning rock.

> In 1679 government forces and the Covenanters fought at the Battle of Drumclog.

Dunaskin

In Gaelic a *dùn* is a hill fort and *ascain* [askan] is the past tense of a rarer Argyll Gaelic word *asgnadh* which means to climb, but that's all speculation and who's asking.

> First, in the mid 19th century, Dunaskin was an ironworks, then in the 20th a brickworks, and then when the demand for bricks fell away, a heritage centre, and now nothing at all.

Dunlop

Named after the tyre inventor? Hardly. It's the other way around. From Gaelic *dùn* (fort) and *lùib* (of the bend), this is fort-on-the-bend.

Fenwick [pronounced fennick]

This seems to be an Old English name, from *fen* (fen) and *wic* (farm, dwelling).

Galston

From Gaelic *gall* [gowl] (foreigner) with the Old English ending *tun* (village). For the Gaels foreigners included Scottish Lowlanders.

Girvan

Two theories: from old Gaelic *gar* (thicket) and *fionn* [fewn] (fair, white). But if the naming source of silver birch clusters doesn't appeal, there is another possibility in Cumbric *gerw* (rough) and *afon* (river). Rough river in current Gaelic would be garbh-abhainn [garav aween] or [garav aveen].

Haugh

Haugh is a Scots word for a river meadow.

Inverkip

From Gaelic *inbhir* [in-yuhr] (river mouth) and old Gaelic *ceap* [k-yep] (top, as in hill top).

Irvine

From Cumbric *yr* (the) and *gwyn* (white), 'the white one' being the (pre-industrial) river.

Kilmarnock

From Gaelic *cill* (church) with *mo Iarnan* [mo ee-uhr-nuhn] (of my Iarnan – a priest) and the diminutive ending *–oc*. The priest's name is also written as Ernoc.

Kilwinning

Ayrshire has a wealth of names deriving from references to early Celtic Christian missionaries. For Kilwinning there is uncertainty as to who exactly the holy man was. Some say it was Finnian, the Irish saint. Gaelic *cill* (church, holy man's cell) accounts for the first part of the name.

Largs

From Gaelic *learg* [leruhg] (hillside). The odd final –s was there in records as long ago as 1140.

In the year 1263 the forces of King Haakon of Norway were repelled here near Largs by Scottish troops under Alexander of Dundonald.

Little Cumbrae

From Cumbric *cymry* (Cumbrians) and Old Norse *ey* (island).

Loudoun

From Scots *lowe* (fire) and Gaelic *dùn* (hill). So a high place for a beacon.

The battle here at Loudoun against the English in 1307 was Robert the Bruce's first significant victory.

Mauchline

From Gaelic *magh* [mahG] (plain) and *linne* [leen-yuh] (pool).

Maybole

This is held to be from Old English *maege* (maiden) and *botl* (house).

The 14th century Crossraguel Abbey lies a couple of miles to the south of Maybole.

Millport

No mystery here. Named after a grain mill at the port.

Minishant

This has nothing to do with size. The name may possibly derive from Gaelic *mòine seunta* [mon-yuh shee-uhntuh] (enchanted peat). A *mòine* can also be a peat-bog and here may refer to the moorland made of peat. So: enchanted moor.

Moscow

This may be from older Gaelic *magh* [mahG] (field) and old Gaelic *coll* [kowl] (hazel).

Ochiltree

From Cumbric *ocel* (high) and *tref* (house).

Patna

The landowner named this place after the Indian city, where he had made his fortune in the early 1800s.

Pinmore

From Gaelic *peighinn* [peh-een-yuh] (land for a penny's rent) and *mòr* (big).

Prestwick

From Old English *preost* (priest) and *wic* (farm).

Saltcoats

The −coats is from Scots *cots* (huts). There were once saltworks here.

Skelmorlie

Just the lea or meadow belonging to someone who had the Old English name of *Scealdamer*.

Sorn

A Gaelic *sòrn* is a kiln, though nowadays the word refers to the flue of a kiln.

Stair

The old Gaelic *stair* [star] means stepping stones or a crossing place over a stream or a bog for cattle or sheep.

Straiton

From Old English *straet* (road) and *tun* (farm or settlement). The straet here probably referred to a Roman road.

Threave

From Cumbric *tref* (settlement, home).

Trearne

A name, not of a settlement now, but a quarry. The name is of a type common in Wales and Cornwall, but rare in Scotland. It comes from Cumbric *tref* (settlement, home) and *àirne* (sloe trees).

Troon

From Cumbric *trwyn* (headland).

Turnberry

The –berry is thought to come from Old Norse *borg* (fort). The Turn– may be from Gaelic *torran* (little hill).

Wemyss Bay [pronounced weems]

This is from Gaelic *uaimh* [oo-Yhv] (cave) but both spelling and pronunciation have become a tad distorted with the passage of time.

Windy Yett

Yett is Scots *yett* which can mean a gate or a pass. So: windy pass.

The Borders
~West

The Eildon Hills

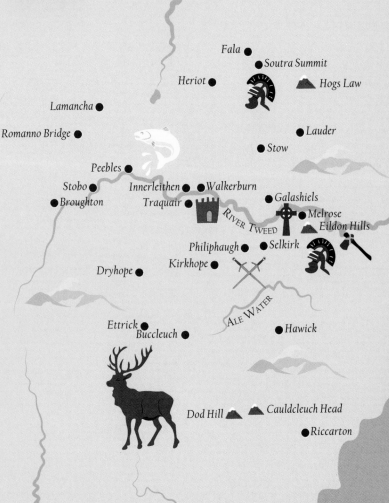

Fala

Soutra Summit

Heriot

Hogs Law

Lamancha

Lauder

Romanno Bridge

Stow

Peebles

Stobo

Innerleithen Walkerburn

Galashiels

Broughton

Traquair

Melrose

RIVER TWEED

Eildon Hills

Philiphaugh Selkirk

Kirkhope

Dryhope

ALE WATER

Ettrick Hawick

Buccleuch

Dod Hill Cauldcleuch Head

Riccarton

Ale Water

The river here does not flow with ale. The Ale here is said to be from an ancient pre-Celtic word for the act of flowing and has also yielded other related river names, like Allan (nearby) and Alness or the Alne down south.

Broughton

From Old English *bróc* (brook) and *tún* (farmstead).

Buccleuch [pronounced buh-klew]

From Old English *buk* (buck) and Middle English *cloghe* (glen).

Cauldcleuch Head

From Scots *cauld* (cold) and *cleuch* (hollow).

Cauldcleuch Head is the only hill in the area that is more than 2000 foot high and that therefore qualifies as a Graham.

Dod Hill

A dod in Scots is a rounded bare-topped hill.

Dryhope

From Old English *dryge* (fort) and *hop* (hollow, valley). *Dryge* can also mean dry.

Eildon Hills

From Gaelic *dùn* (hill fort) preceded by an old Gaelic word *àill* (rock).

At the foot of the triple-peaked Eildons are the remains of a Roman camp. Trimontium was the Roman name for these impressive hills, known to have been a centre since Bronze-Age days.

Ettrick

Named after the river, Ettrick Water. Some say, a little less than helpfully, that Gaelic *eadar* [etuh] (between) might be involved here. Alternatively Cumbric *atre* (playful) might be behind things as a likely description of flowing and burbling water. On the other hand, the name, as with many river names, may well track back into pre-recorded days.

Fala

From an older Gaelic sense of *fàl* (enclosure for sheep or cattle) and the ending *–ach* [ahK] indicating a place. So: sheepfold or cattle pen.

Galashiels

Shielins by the Gala Water (a shielin being a hut used by a herdsman).

Hawick [pronounced hoyk]

From Old English *haga* (hedge) and *wic* (settlement). The surrounding hedge is unsurprisingly no longer a feature.

Heriot

From Old English *here* (army) and *geat* (pass). This was a pass through which an army could march.

Hogs Law

Law is a Scots word for hill, a rounded hill, and this part of the country is full of laws. Law is related to Old English *hlaew* (hill).

Innerleithen

There is no Outerleithen because inner here comes from Gaelic *inbhir* [in-yuhr] meaning confluence. This is where the river Leithen joins the Tweed. (The Gaelic normally turned into inver not inner.)

Kirkhope

Originally nothing to do with hope. *Hop* is an Old English word for valley or hollow; and kirk, deriving from Old English *ciric* is, of course, still modern Scots for church.

Lamancha

Spanish? Yes, the local landowner decided to call it that back in 1730.

Lauder

Possibly named after the river: Cumbric *lou* (wash) and (Cumbric or old Gaelic) *dobhar* [doh-wuhr] (water).

Melrose

Guess at honey and roses? No, much bleaker. It's bare moor. From Cumbric *mailo* (bare) and *ros* (moor).

Peebles

From Cumbric *pebyll* (tents).

Philiphaugh

No ancient Philip involved here. It's from Old English *ful* (closed) and *hop* (valley). Haugh is a Scots word for a river meadow. All in all a pretty precise geographical name: closed valley river meadow.

> The Battle of Philiphaugh was fought in 1645 between Covenanters and Royalists.

Riccarton

This is just Richard's *ton* or settlement.

Romanno Bridge

Nothing to do with gypsies. It's from Gaelic *ràth* [ra] (ring-fort) and *manaich* [maneeK] (of the monk).

Selkirk

From Old English *sele* (manor house) and *ciric*, which became Scots kirk.

Soutra Summit

From Cumbric *sulw* (view) and *tref* (homestead). So: a home with a view.

> Just south of Soutra and by the B6368 is a stretch of Roman road, called Dere Street, still looking like a road after nearly 2000 years.

Stobo

From Old English *stub* (stump) and *how* (hollow). *Howe* is also Scots for a hollow. So: a hollow with tree stumps in it.

Stow

From Old English *stow* which simply means town or place. A fairly minimalist description.

Traquair

From Cumbric *tref* (settlement, home) and the river name Quair, possibly from Cumbric *vedra* (clear one).

Tweed, River

Possibly derived from the same root form as Tay, a form meaning strong and silent. River names are generally of very ancient descent and with a meaning (if they had one) lost in the mists of time.

> *The River Tweed is historically a boundary between England and Scotland.*

Walkerburn

A walker here is someone who waulks cloth, that is someone who works at scouring and thickening cloth. And the mills tended to be by burns or streams.

The Borders
~ East

Smailholm Tower

Penmanshiel Tunnel

Eyemouth

Reston

Ayton

Longformacus

Whitchester

Duns

Polwarth

RIVER TWEED

Thirlestane

Boon

Gordon

Earlston

Floors Castle

Coldstream

Redpath

Kelso

Dryburgh

Rutherford

Roxburgh

Kirk Yetholm
Town Yetholm

Ancrum

Morebattle

Jedburgh

Cessford

Denholm

Bedrule

Abbotrule

Hobkirk

Chesters

Abbotrule

Just what it says: the area ruled by the abbot.

Ancrum

The *crum* is a Cumbric word for bend related to *crom* in Gaelic which has the same meaning. *An* is Gaelic for the.

> *The Battle of Ancrum Moor was fought in 1545 as part of what is known as the War of the Rough Wooing. It was a victory for the Scots who objected to the plan to marry off Mary Queen of Scots (to be) to the English throne.*

Ayton

Named after the river, which is called Eye in modern English, from Old English *éa* (running water) and *tun* (farmstead).

Bedrule

The land ruled over by a certain *Bethóc* in distant days. The name has been worn down with the passage of time.

Boon

Not as idealistically positive as it might sound, this name is quite probably from the Gaelic *bonn* [bown] which means bottom, as in the bottom of a hill.

Cessford

A ford through a cess pool? No, this has mutated a bit. It is from Old English *worth* (an enclosed field) and the personal name *Cessa*.

Chesters

There are not many Chesters in Scotland, while England has hordes. This comes from the plural form *castra* of Latin *castrum* (camp) via Old English *ceastra*.

Coldstream

Just what it says on the tin. This was a fording place before the bridge was built; and the stream was cold.

Denholm

From Old English *denu* (valley) and *holmr* (island).

Dryburgh

Not that there are no pubs. Not dry, the name's from Old English *dryge* (fort) and *burh* (town).

> *Dryburgh is the burial place of Sir Walter Scott.*

Duns

From Gaelic *dùn* [doon] (hill, fort). The English plural ending could come from the fact that the original dun was destroyed then rebuilt.

> *Some 5 miles north of Duns is the Iron-Age fortress, Edin's Hall Broch.*

Earlston

Not an earl's town. *Earcil* was a person's name back in the 11th century and *dun* is Old English for hill.

Eyemouth

Eye comes from Old English *éa* meaning river.

Floors Castle

Not floors but flowers. And the building that preceded the stately home on this site was called House of Floris.

Gordon

From Cumbric *gor* (great) and *din* (fort).

Hobkirk

From Old English *hop* (valley, hollow) and *ciric* which became Scots *kirk* (church).

Jedburgh

The burgh or town by the Jed, the river name coming, it is thought, from Cumbric *gweden* (to wind).

Kelso

From Old English *calc* (chalk) and *how* (hill). The name was recorded as Calkou in 1126.

> *The 15th century Smailholm Tower (a peel tower) stands 6 miles west of Kelso.*

Longformacus

From old Gaelic or Cumbric *lann* [lown] (church), *fothir* [fohir] (land) and *Maccus* (a personal name). So: church on Maccus' land.

Morebattle

Nothing to do with a historic battle. This comes either from Gaelic *mòr* (big) and Old English *botl* (house) or from Old English *mor* (moor) plus Old English *botl*. This latter is more likely since the Gaelic ought to have yielded Battlemore.

Penmanshiel Tunnel

The tunnel, now blocked up, has an ancient and mixed name, from Cumbric *pen* (head, top), *maen* (stone) and the Scots *shiel* (summer grazing land).

Polwarth

From Old English *worth* (field) coming after the personal name *Pol*.

Redpath

This is often said to be no more than the sum of its parts, being in Old English a *reâd pæþ*, a path that is red in colour. But maybe it could also be traceable to Old English *riht* (straight) or indeed to what the Danes, who were active and influential not too far from here, would call *ret* (straight).

Reston

From a Cumbric personal name *Rhys* and Old English *tun* (farm).

Roxburgh

Hroc is a personal name in Old English. And the burgh was his fortress.

Rutherford

Old English *hrythera* were horned cattle. Here they could ford.

Thirlestane

From Old English *thyrel* (hole) and *stan* (stone). It could have been named after its millstone.

Tweed, River

Possibly derived from the same root form as Tay, a form meaning strong and silent. River names are generally of very ancient descent and with a meaning (if they had one) lost in the mists of time.

> *The River Tweed is historically a boundary between England and Scotland.*

Whitchester

A rarity in Scotland, this is placename testimony to Roman presence with their 'chester' (Latin *castra*) or camp to which the Old English adjective *hwit* (white) was prefixed.

Yetholm, (Town and Kirk) [pronounced yettam]

From Old English *geat* (pass, gate) which became Scots *yett*. In other parts of Scotland the *holmr* would be Old Norse for island, but older versions of this name have the ending as *ham*, which is Old English for village. And the fact that the pronunciation is [yettam] should settle the matter.

Dumfries &
Galloway
~West

Loch Ryan

Pinwherry

Ballantrae

Loch Moan

Lochinvar

Dalry

Bogue

New Galloway

Clatteringshaws Loch

Risk (Farm)

River Fleet

The Lane

Loch Ken

Loch Ryan

Cairnryan

New Luce

Challoch

Newton Stewart

Minnigaff

River Dee

Stranraer

Tarf Water

Glenluce

Gatehouse of Fleet

Wigtown

Tongland

Portpatrick

Elrig

Sorbie

Kirkcudbright

Borgue

Ross

Balgowan

Whithorn

Balgowan

From Gaelic *baile* [baluh] (homestead, place) the *ghobhainn* [Goh-een] (of the blacksmith).

Ballantrae

This could be from Gaelic *baile* [baluh] (homestead, village), *na tràgha* [trah-Guh] (by the shore, by the beach).

Bogue

Possibly from Gaelic *bog* which is an adjective meaning boggy. The –ue lends the Gaelic a certain Gallic tone.

Borgue

No connection with the similar-looking placename of Bogue. This is from Old Norse *borg* meaning a fortified place. And, as with Borgue, the –ue ending gives a certain French tone.

Cairnryan

From Cumbric *caer* (fort) and *rigon* (chief's).

Challoch

From Gaelic *teallach* [chelloch] (forge, anvil).

Clatteringshaws, Loch

Shaw is Scots for wood, as is Old English *sceaga*. The Clattering– may be an Old Norse admixture, *klettr* being a cliff or rocky outcrop.

Dalry

From Gaelic *dail* [dal] (field) and *fhraoich* [rur-eeK] (heather). Or the –ry element (which takes the stress) may be from Gaelic *ruighe* [ree-yuh] (lower slope).

Dee, River

The belief is that this name is related to Gaelic *dia* (god). In ancient times rivers were seen as having divine status.

Elrig

Likely from an old Gaelic word *eilreig* [elrek] (ambush), the ambush being a narrow or enclosed space which acted as a trap for finishing off hunted deer that were driven into it.

Elrig is the birthplace of naturalist and author Gavin Maxwell.

And just to the south of Elrig is the Iron-Age settlement of Barsalloch Fort. This whole area abounds with standing stones.

Fleet, River

From Old English *fleot* (estuary).

Gatehouse of Fleet

No gate involved here. This is from Old English *geata-hus*, which means roadhouse. The Fleet's the river.

Cardoness Castle stands high up overlooking Fleet Bay a mile southwest of Gatehouse of Fleet.

Glenluce

The –luce is from Gaelic *lus*, which means herb.

Ken, Loch

Old Gaelic *càin* [kahn] means white.

Kirkcudbright

[pronounced kirkoobree]
Kirk is Scots for church, related to both Old Norse *kirkja* and Old English *ciric*, and Cudbright is the name, much altered, of the 7th century English saint Cuthbert, who became Bishop of Lindisfarne. The Old English version of his name is Cudberct.

The remains of the 16th century MacLellan's Castle stand in the centre of Kirkcudbright.

Lane, The

The name of this stretch of water at the northern end of Loch Ken is thought to come from the Gaelic *linne* [leen-yuh] (pond).

Lochinvar

From Gaelic *an bharra* [uhn varra] (at the height).

Minnigaff

Not a small mistake, this is said to come, with multiple twists and contortions, from Gaelic *monadh* [monuhG] (hill, moor) and *a' ghobhainn* [uh-Goh-een] (of the smith). So: Smithhill.

Moan, Loch

This is very probably a lugubriously anglicized remnant of the Gaelic *mòine* [mon-yuh] which means peat.

New Galloway

Galloway is from Gaelic *Gall* and *Ghàidheil* [Gay-yehl] (foreign Gaels). The district is referred to as Galweya in the Pictish Chronicle sometime around AD 970. The Gaels who once lived here were of mixed Irish and Norse stock and considered foreigners by their northern neighbours.

New Luce

Italian for light? No, from Gaelic *lus*, which means herb. So: new herb garden.

Newton Stewart

Just what it says, the Stewarts' new town.

Pinwherry

From Gaelic *peighinn* [peh-een-yuh] (land for a penny's rent) and *an fhoithre* [uhn oyruh] (of the copse). The Gaelic pronunciation was clearly too much of a headache for the informants and scribes of the day.

Portpatrick

This little port was named in honour of St Patrick, patron saint of Ireland and was once the main port for traffic to and from Ireland, the coast of Ireland being visible from here.

Risk (Farm)

From Gaelic *riasg* [ree-uhsg] meaning bog or marsh. Risk occurs as a name element in various parts of Scotland, often in association with farms and homesteads which didn't grow into towns.

Ross

From old Gaelic *ros* (promontory, moor). What does the landscape suggest?

Ryan, Loch

Possibly from Cumbric *rigon* (chief), which is related to Welsh *rhion*, which has the same meaning.

Sorbie

From Old Norse (or Danish) *saur* (bog) and *bú* (settlement). Was this a settlement on or near a bog? Perhaps the bog afforded some protection.

Stranraer

From Gaelic *sròn* [stron] (nose, point) and *reamhar* [rafuhr] (fat). Look at it on the map to see why it got this name.

Tarf Water

From Gaelic *tarbh* [tarav] which means bull.

Tongland

This name just means a bit of land shaped like a tongue (Old English *tunge*).

Whithorn

From Old English *hwit* (white) and *erne* (house).

Whithorn Priory stands on the ground where Scotland's first converts to Christianity came to worship.

Wigtown

From the Old English personal name *Wicga* and *tun* (farm).

A Bronze-Age stone circle, called Torhouse, stands some 4 miles to the west of Wigtown.

This sleepy little place is nowadays called Scotland's Book Town and hosts an annual book festival. Around the main square just about every other door leads into a bookshop, secondhand and new.

Dumfries & Galloway ~East

Grey Mare's Tail, Moffat Hills

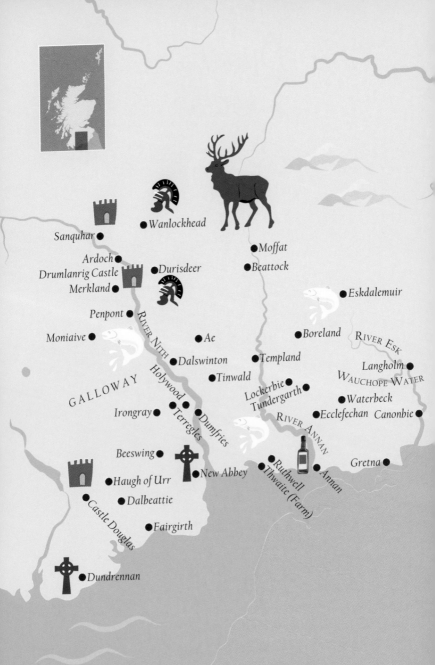

Ae [pronounced ay]

This, one of the country's shortest placenames, comes from Old Norse *á* (river). The village did not exist before 1947; the forest is older; but the name originated, as you might expect, with the river.

Annan (town and river)

Theories: *Anu* was a Celtic goddess of fertility and prosperity and was also known as *Anann*. Also: *an* is an old Gaelic word for water and −*an* is a diminutive ending.

Ardoch

From Gaelic *àrdach* [ahrtoK] (high place).

Beattock

From Gaelic *biodach* [beedoK] (sharp-peaked, like a pyramid).

Beeswing

Named after a 19th century racehorse, called Beeswing. Well, they move fast.

Boreland

The boring bit is thought to originate with Old English *bord*, which, as in the expression 'board and lodging', refers to the provision of food, making this land farmed to feed the landlord.

Canonbie

Probably from Nordic *bú* (dwelling, village) with canon, referring to the canon of the old Augustinian priory here. But here the −bie is quite likely to point to Danes, or Danish influence, coming from the east.

Castle Douglas

The name Douglas is thought to derive from the Gaelic *dubh* [doo] (dark) and an old Gaelic sense of *glas* (water, stream).

The Douglas family castle is called Threave and is situated some 3 miles to the west of Castle Douglas. It was built in the 1370s by Archibald Douglas, known as The Grim. The name Threave is derived from the Cumbric word tref meaning homestead.

Dalbeattie

From Gaelic *dail* [dal] (field) and *beitheach* [beh-hoK] (of birches). So: Birchfield.

Dalswinton

A mixture. From Gaelic *dail* [dal] (field) and Old English *swin* (pig) and *tun* (farmstead). Probably a Gaelic prefix was stuck onto an existing English name.

Drumlanrig Castle

From the Gaelic *druim* [droo-im] (ridge) and a Cumbric word *llanerch* (clearing).

Dumfries

From Gaelic *dùn* (hill fort) and *phris* [freesh] (of the woodland).

The burial place of Robert Burns is in Dumfries in the churchyard of St Michael's.

Dundrennan

From the Gaelic *dùn* (hill) and *droighnean* [droynyen] (of thorns).

In 1568 Mary Queen of Scots spent her last night ever in Scotland here at the abbey in Dundrennan, before travelling south to England.

Durisdeer

The name has no reference to deer. Starting from the back, the –deer is from Gaelic *doire* [doruh] (grove, copse); the –ris– is thought to be an older Gaelic sense of *ros* (wood); and the Dur– is thought to be from Gaelic *dubh* [doo] (dark, black). So we have the copse of the dark wood. Repetitiveness is not that uncommon in placenames, especially where one element may have ceased to have a meaning.

A Roman road ran right through the place where the little village of Durisdeer now stands. And the recognizable remains of Roman camps can be seen nearby.

Ecclefechan

There are two theories about this name. One is that it derives from Fechin, the name of a 7th century Irish evangelizer of the Scots and the Gaelic *eaglais* [ek-lish] (church). The other theory has it coming from earlier Cumbric words *egles fychan* (little church).

Little Ecclefechan, past which the M74 motorway now carries its rushing traffic, has its claim to fame in that Thomas Carlyle, historian, writer and philosopher, was born here in 1795. The description of economics as the dismal science is attributed to him.

Esk, River

From an ancient Celtic word *easg* (river). Gaelic *uisge* [oosh-guh] (water) is cognate.

Eskdalemuir

The moor of the Esk valley.

Fairgirth

Possibly a cultural mixture, from old Gaelic *gart* (field) together with Old Norse *fær* (sheep).

Galloway

Referred to as Galweya in the Pictish Chronicle of around AD 970, this is what northern Gaels called the land of the *Gall Ghàidheil* [Gay-yehl] (foreign Gaels), foreign because part Irish and part Norse.

Gretna

Poossibly from Old English *greoten* (gravelly) and *halth* (fertile land by a river, a haugh in Scots).

An English marriage act passed in 1753 required parental consent for a couple under 21 years of age to marry; not so in libertarian Scotland where laddies of 14 and lassies of 12 could get married if they wanted. Gretna is just across the border and became a favourite place to elope to; and it still does a good wedding business these days.

Haugh of Urr

A haugh is a waterside meadow (in Scots) and the Urr is the river name, the Urr Water, a very ancient river name, going back to times before the Celts.

Holywood

Originally called Darcongall, the wood (Gaelic *doire*) of St Congall. With the founding of the 12th century abbey here an English name took over. Holy means just that, it was a holy place.

Irongray

Not a former smelting works. From Gaelic *earrann* [yar-uhn] (area) *na greigh* [na gray] (of the stud or of the herd of deer).

Langholm [pronounced lang-um]

From Scots *lang* (long) and *holm* (water meadow), the *holm* being cognate with Old Norse *holmr*, which can mean both a small island and a waterside meadow.

Lockerbie

From Old Norse *Lokard* (a name) and *bú* (dwelling, village). A document dated 1306 has this now sadly famous place as Lokardebi.

Merkland

A merk was a unit of currency used in Scotland towards the end of the 16th century and during the 17th century. This was land rented for a merk.

Moffat

From Gaelic *magh* [mahG] (field) and *fada* (long).

Moffat was an important stopping-off point on the road between England and Scotland before the motorway swept past.

Moniaive

From Gaelic *mòine* [mon-yuh] (peat, peat bog) and *èibhe* [ayvuh] (cry). Mysterious.

New Abbey

This village gets its name from its abbey, which was new in 1273.

> *Sweetheart Abbey, near New Abbey, was founded by Lady Devorguilla of Galloway, although it wasn't called this at the time. When she died Lady Devorguilla, who was the mother of Scotland's King John, was buried by the high altar here next to the embalmed heart of her beloved dead husband, John de Balliol. It was the monks who gave the abbey this name.*

Nith, River

From Cumbric *nedd* (glistening). The name, related to Neath in South Wales, stems from the sparkling and glistening waters of the stream that flowed here.

Penpont

From Cumbric *pen* (head, top) and *pont* (bridge). These are remains of linguistic forms that spread more widely in Wales. In Scotland *pen*– became *ceann*– hence kin–.

Ruthwell

From Old English *róde* (cross) and *well* (well).

> *In Ruthwell you can still see the Celtic cross which dates from the late 7th or early 8th century.*

Sanquhar [pronounced sanker]

From Gaelic *sean* [shen] (old) and Cumbric *caer* (fort).

Templand

Not a recruitment agency centre. The land here used to belong to the Knights Templar.

Terregles

Place with a church. From Cumbric *egles* (church), with obvious French connections, and the prefix which is commoner in Wales, *tre*– for homestead or village.

Thwaite (Farm)

This is a fairly common name element in the north of England but relatively rare in Scotland, although there are some related Twatts a long way further north. It's from Old Norse þveit (clearing, hence settlement). Here it survives as the name of a farm.

Tinwald

It's tempting to look for German connections with *Wald* (forest). But this is from Old Norse þing (parliament, assembly) and *vǫllr* (field). A place where people met to settle issues.

Tundergarth

Two views. Either from Gaelic *tòrr a' ghaoth* [tor uh gur] (windy hill). Or, more entertainingly, from Gaelic *tòn* (backside) and *ri gaoith* [ree gur-ee] (to the wind).

Wanlockhead

Wanlock Water is from Cumbric *gwyn* (white) and *llech* (flat stone). The English –head was added to mark the site of the village at the head of the stream.

> *Wanlockhead has been a mining site for lead, silver and gold since Roman times and before.*

Waterbeck

One theory is that the name comes from Old Norse *vatn* (water) and *bekkr* (stream). There are lots of becks in the Lake District in the north of England, but not many at all in Scotland. And who would call a place water stream? The beck could also be from Gaelic *beag* [bek] (little).

Wauchope Water

From Old English *walc* or *wealh* (foreigner, outsider) and *hop* (hollow). As Galloway was seen as the home of foreign Gaels this district was a valley of outsiders, sundry travellers settling down.

DIY Placenames

On your travels around Scotland, in your car or armchair, on your bike, feet or boat, you are going to come across many more placenames than are listed and accounted for in this book.

So here is the DIY or Derive-It-Yourself section. But handle with care, derive with caution, things are not always what they seem. Hundreds of years ago names may have been misheard, miscopied, misspelled, written down by a short-sighted or hard-of-hearing scribe or cobbled together into something resembling something that the scribe might recognize as a word when straining to make out the alien utterances of a Gaelic-speaking villager, who in his or her turn, may have learnt the name from his or her great-grandmother, who herself based it roughly on what was said to her in her youth by a one-time Viking settler.

Name elements occurring in first position can, of course, also be checked against this book's index.

present-day name element

ORIGINATING LANGUAGE
how written in that language
meaning

-**a** OLD NORSE *ey* island
 or OLD NORSE *á* river
a- GAELIC *àth* ford
-**ab** GAELIC *aba* abbot
aber- BRITTONIC-PICTISH confluence; river mouth
ach- GAELIC *achadh* field
-**ach** OLD GAELIC -*ach* ending indicating a place
af- OLD GAELIC *àbh* stream
-**aidh** GAELIC an ending indicating place
-**aig** OLD NORSE *vík* bay
aird GAELIC *àird* height, headland

237

aith Old Norse *eið* isthmus, tongue

-al Old Norse *fjall* hill

al- old Gaelic *ail* rock

aline Gaelic *àlainn* beautiful

alt Gaelic *allt* stream

-am Old Norse *holmr* small island
  or Old English *holm* waterside meadow

-an Gaelic *-an* little

annet old Gaelic *annaid* church

ard Gaelic *àrd* high

arm Old Norse *armr* arm

as Old Norse *áss* ridge

-as Gaelic *-ais* ending which indicates place

auch- Gaelic *achadh* field

auchter- Gaelic *uachdar* upland

auld Gaelic *allt* stream

avon Gaelic *abhainn* river

-ay Old Norse *ey* island

ay- Old English *éa* running water

back Old Norse *bakki* bank
  or Gaelic *bac* hollow

bad- Gaelic *bad* thicket

bal-, bale-, bali-, balla-, bally Gaelic *baile* homestead,
  farm (modern Gaelic for town)

ban- Gaelic *banbh* pig

bar- Gaelic *bàrr* top

battle Old English *botl* house

beck Old Norse *bekkr* stream

-beg Gaelic *beag* little

beath, beith Gaelic *beithe* birch

ben Gaelic *beinn* mountain

ber Old English *bere* barley

-bie Old Norse *bú* settlement

big OLD NORSE bygg barley

-bister OLD NORSE bólstaðr homestead, farm

blair GAELIC blàr field, plain

blan CUMBRIC blaen edge

-ble OLD NORSE ból(staðr) farm, homestead

bog GAELIC bog boggy

-bol(l) OLD NORSE ból(staðr) farm

bon- GAELIC bonn bottom

borg, borro- OLD NORSE borg fort

-bost OLD NORSE bólstaðr homestead, farm

brac OLD NORSE brekkr slope

brae GAELIC bràigh upland

-breac GAELIC breac trout

brig OLD ENGLISH brycg bridge
  (from which) SCOTS brig bridge

brox OLD ENGLISH broccs badger's

-buie GAELIC buidhe yellow

bun- GAELIC bonn bottom

burn OLD ENGLISH burna stream

bur(r) OLD NORSE borg fort

-busta OLD NORSE bólstaðr homestead, farm

-by OLD NORSE bú farm

cairn GAELIC càrn hill; cairn
  or BRITTONIC cardden wood

cait CUMBRIC OR BRITTONIC coet wood

calder, -caldy BRITTONIC caled hard

-call OLD GAELIC coll hazel tree

cambus GAELIC camas bay, landing place

caple GAELIC capall horse

car CUMBRIC OR BRITTONIC caer fort

carden BRITTONIC-PICTISH cardden wood, thicket

-caul OLD GAELIC coll hazel tree

chon OLD GAELIC chon of dogs, of wolves

-chulish GAELIC caolas narrows

clachan GAELIC clachan stones; hamlet; churchyard

clack- GAELIC clach stone

clash GAELIC clais ditch, trench

clatt OLD NORSE klettr cliff, rocky outcrop

-clete GAELIC cleite rocky outcrop

cloich GAELIC clach stone

cow OLD GAELIC coll hazel

craig GAELIC creag rock

crieff GAELIC craobh tree

crom GAELIC crom bent

-crum GAELIC crom bend

cul GAELIC cuil corner

dal GAELIC dail field, meadow

dal(e) OLD NORSE dalr valley

-darroch GAELIC darach oak

-deer GAELIC doire grove

-den, denny OLD ENGLISH denu valley

ding OLD NORSE þing parliament, assembly

do-, du- GAELIC dubh dark, black

doll- OLD GAELIC dol meadow

doun(e) GAELIC dùn hill fort

-dour OLD GAELIC dobhar water

-dow GAELIC dubh dark, black

drum GAELIC druim ridge

-dry CUMBRIC tref village

dum-, dun- GAELIC dùn fort

eagles GAELIC eaglais church

eccle GAELIC eaglais church

edin GAELIC aodann hillface
   or CUMBRIC eidynn rockface

-es GAELIC -ais ending which indicates place

ewe OLD GAELIC iù yew tree

240

fair Old Norse fær sheep

fal old Gaelic fàl enclosure for sheep or cattle

fas old Gaelic fas place

fearn Gaelic feàrna alders

fetter- old Gaelic faithir slope

fin- Gaelic fionn white, fair

fit- old Gaelic fòid peat

fors Old Norse fors waterfall

foul Old Norse fugl bird

-four Gaelic phùir of the crop land

-foyle Gaelic phuill pool

-ful Old Norse fjall hill

gair- Gaelic geàrr short

gal Gaelic gall foreigner

gar Gaelic gàrradh garden
  or Gaelic garbh rough

gare Gaelic geàrr short

garra Old Norse garðr enclosure
  or Gaelic gàrradh enclosure

gart(h) old Gaelic gart field

gask old Gaelic gasg tail (of land)

gate Cumbric or Brittonic coed wood

gate Old English geata road
  (from which) Scots gait road

-gay Gaelic gaoithe of the wind

glas old Gaelic glas water, stream
  or Gaelic or Brittonic glas green

-goe Old Norse gjá geo (steep-sided inlet)

-gow Cumbric cau hollow

-gown Gaelic ghobhainn smith's

hal Gaelic coille wood
  or Old Norse hár high

-ham Old English ham village

-hannet OLD GAELIC annaid church

haugh OLD NORSE haugr mound
  or SCOTS haugh water meadow

her- OLD ENGLISH here army

hob OLD ENGLISH hop valley, hollow

holm OLD NORSE holmr small island
  or OLD ENGLISH holm waterside meadow

hope OLD NORSE hóp bay
  or OLD ENGLISH hop hollow, valley

how(e) OLD NORSE haugr mound
  or SCOTS howe hollow

-ie GAELIC -aidh ending which indicates place

inch GAELIC innis island; water-meadow.

-ing- OLD ENGLISH ing the people of

inner GAELIC inbhir confluence; river mouth

inver- GAELIC inbhir river mouth; confluence

iron GAELIC earrann portion of land

kel GAELIC caol narrow

kel- GAELIC caol narrow

kell GAELIC ceall holy man's cell

-kell GAELIC coille wood

kem, ken GAELIC ceann head

kil- GAELIC cill holy man's cell, sometimes church
  or GAELIC caol narrow

killie- GAELIC coille wood

kin- GAELIC cinn at the head of

kip OLD GAELIC ceap top

kir- BRITTONIC-PICTISH caer fort

kirk OLD NORSE kirkja church

knap- OLD NORSE knappr knob, lumpy hill

knock GAELIC cnoc hill

kyle GAELIC caol narrows, strait
  or GAELIC coille wood

lag Gaelic lag hollow

laggan Gaelic lagan little hollow

lairg Old Gaelic làirig pass

-lang Gaelic long of ships

lann Cumbric lann enclosure

-larich Old Gaelic làirig pass

-latur Old Gaelic leitir hillside

law Old English hlaew hill
  (from which) Scots law hill

lax Old Norse lax salmon

leck Gaelic leac flagstone; gravestone

les Gaelic lios garden

-let Gaelic leathad slope

letter- Gaelic leitir hillside

leven Gaelic leamhain elms

lin Old Norse lín flax
  or Gaelic lìon flax

linn Old Gaelic linne falls

loch Old Gaelic lòch black, dark (as well, of course, as the modern sense)

logie Gaelic lagaigh hollow place

long Gaelic long, luing ship, of ships
  or Old Gaelic lann enclosure; churchland

luce Gaelic lus herb

mal- Old Norse múli headland

mag-, mauch- Gaelic magh plain; field

mara Gaelic mara of the sea

mel- Cumbric mailo bare
  or Old Norse melr grassy dune
  or Gaelic meall mountain

mo- Gaelic magh plain; field

mon(t) Gaelic monadh hill, moor
  or Gaelic mòine peat

more GAELIC mòr big

muck GAELIC muc pig

muir GAELIC Mhoire Mary's
  or OLD ENGLISH, SCOTS muir moor

na GAELIC na of the

-nis(h) OLD NORSE nes headland

ob GAELIC òb bay
  or OLD NORSE hóp bay

-och GAELIC ach indicates place

ochter GAELIC uachdar upland

ord OLD GAELIC òrd rounded hill

otter GAELIC oitir sandbar

pab- OLD NORSE papa priest, missionary monk

pen- CUMBRIC pen head

pein- GAELIC peighinn land for a penny's rent

pett PICTISH pit (piece of) land

pin- GAELIC peighinn land for a penny's rent

pit PICTISH pit (piece of) land

pol- GAELIC poll pool

-pol, -pool OLD NORSE ból farm

-quhar CUMBRIC caer fort

qui-, quoy OLD NORSE kví cattle pen

ra-, rath-, -reay GAELIC ràth circular fort

-res OLD GAELIC ros wood

rhu- GAELIC rubha headland

-rie GAELIC ruighe slope

ros OLD GAELIC ros cape; wood

rose OLD GAELIC ros headland; wood

ross OLD GAELIC OR CUMBRIC ros promontory

ruth GAELIC ruadh red

scarp OLD NORSE skarfr cormorant
  or OLD NORSE skárpr barren

scour- OLD NORSE skógr wood

-setter, -shader Old Norse *sætr* homestead

shaw Old English *sceaga* wood
  or Old Norse *skógr* wood
  or Old Norse *sjá* sea loch

shee Gaelic *sìth* peace; fairy

-sheen Gaelic *sine* nipple

-sie Gaelic *sìth* hill; fairy

skaill Old Norse *skáli* large cottage; hall

skaw, -sker Old Norse *sker* prominent rock

skip- Old Norse *skip* ship

sor- Old Norse *saur* bog

stan(e) Old English *stan* stone

-sta Old Norse *staðr*, homestead, dwelling

sten Old Norse *steinn* stone

-ster Old Norse *bólstaðr* homestead, farm

stra; strath Gaelic *srath* wide river valley

stran- Gaelic *sròn* nose, point

strom Old Norse *straumr* current

stron- Gaelic *sròn* nose, point

suie Gaelic *suidhe* seat

sword Old Norse *svarð* grassy sward

taing Old Norse *tangi* spit, tongue of land

tarbert Gaelic *tairbeart* isthmus, portage point

tarf, tarv Gaelic *tarbh* bull

tay Gaelic *taigh* house

-ter Gaelic *tìr* land

tibber, -tiber Gaelic *tobar* well

tilli-, tilly- Gaelic *tulach* hill, hillock

ting- Old Norse *þing* parliament, assembly

-tinny Gaelic *teine* fire

tober- Gaelic *tobar* well

-tocher old Gaelic *tochar* causeway, roadway

toft Old Norse *toft* homestead; building site

tom- GAELIC tom hillock

-ton OLD ENGLISH tun farmstead
  or GAELIC donn brown

tor- GAELIC tòrr hill, mound

tot- OLD NORSE toft homestead; building site

tough GAELIC tulach hill

-toul GAELIC t-sabhail barn's

tra-, -tray, -try CUMBRIC OR BRITTONIC tref settlement, homestead

-try GAELIC tìr land

tulli-, tully GAELIC tulach hill, hillock

turc, turk GAELIC turc boar

ty GAELIC taigh house

-ty GAELIC dia goddess

-tyre GAELIC tìr land

uig OLD NORSE vík bay

-vaig OLD NORSE vík bay

-val OLD NORSE fjall hill

-vanich GAELIC mhanaich of the monk

vat OLD NORSE vatn water
  or OLD NORSE vátr wet

-ven, -vin GAELIC abhainn river

-voe OLD NORSE vágr bay, inlet

-wall OLD NORSE vǫllr field

-warth OLD ENGLISH worth enclosure

-way OLD NORSE vágr bay

whit OLD ENGLISH hwit white

-wick OLD ENGLISH wic farm, dwelling
  or OLD NORSE vík bay

yett OLD ENGLISH geata gate; pass
  (from which) SCOTS yett gate; pass

Index